Praise for **Listen to Sell**

"At last, a refreshingly different book about selling that elevates the role of sales to the level it deserves. We applaud the authors' emphasis on the process of building trust via genuine listening. *Listen to Sell* identifies solid research and then makes it practical and applicable. It is the new bible for those aspiring to succeed at this noble profession."

JOHN ZENGER & JOSEPH FOLKMAN, coauthors of *The New Extraordinary Leader*

"Listening is the secret sauce of successful sales—and this book unveils the recipe for mastering it. *Listen to Sell* is a must-read for anyone looking to create loyal customers."

KEN BLANCHARD, coauthor of *The One Minute Manager* and *Raving Fans*

"Mike Esterday and Derek Roberts know more about sales than anyone I know. *Listen to Sell* has all the tools you need to make yourself a better salesperson."

DR. TRAVIS BRADBERRY, bestselling author of *Emotional Intelligence Habits*

"The best salespeople are dedicated to making a difference and improving the lives of customers. Mike Esterday and Derek Roberts spell out clearly why selling, at its heart, is about establishing your true purpose and unlocking your internal drivers. *Listen to Sell* helps you have the right conversations with yourself, and then teaches you how to carry that sense of purpose into your conversations with your customers."

LISA EARLE MCLEOD, bestselling author of *Selling with Noble Purpose*

"In sales, there's a time to talk and there's a time to listen. Get that right, and you get the sale. Get it wrong, and you get frustration. This practical book shows you how to get it right."

MICHAEL BUNGAY STANIER, author of *The Coaching Habit* and *How to Work with (Almost) Anyone*

"*Listen to Sell* is a timely reminder that selling doesn't happen until we listen first to our customers. My father, Stephen R. Covey, put it this way: 'Seek first to understand, then to be understood.' Asking great questions is important but useless if we haven't learned to listen. Mike Esterday and Derek Roberts show us why being an emotionally intelligent salesperson, one who diagnoses (listens) before prescribing (offering our solution), is essential for enduring success as sales professionals."

DAVID M.R. COVEY, CEO of SMCOVEY and bestselling coauthor of *Trap Tales*

"A valuable primer and welcome reminder of the uniquely human factors that make the difference in sales. *Listen to Sell* helps you tap into the mindset, skillset, and strategies to show up with confidence and break through to new levels of performance. Best of all, it's grounded in a set of principles that reinforces the value you bring to the table and will make you proud to be part of the sales profession."

KARIN HURT, founder and CEO of Let's Grow Leaders

"Effective selling today is all about actively listening to clients to find out their goals and objectives and then—and only then—creating customized solutions. *Listen to Sell* is an excellent book to help you deliver superior selling experiences through the power of listening."

DR. TONY ALESSANDRA, coauthor of *The Platinum Rule* and *Communicating at Work*

"The results we achieve in sales begins with our mindset and how we prepare. *Listen to Sell* is the step-by-step guide every salesperson needs to be successful in today's market. You don't read this book, you apply it."

MARK HUNTER, The Sales Hunter

"Listening creates more successful conversations. *Listen to Sell* outlines the conversations you need to have with yourself and your customers. When you listen more and deepen these conversations, satisfaction and sales success will follow. Listen to me—read this book!"

KEVIN EIKENBERRY, chief potential officer at the Kevin Eikenberry Group and author of *Remarkable Leadership*

"*Listen to Sell* is a groundbreaking exploration into the heart of authentic selling. This book stands out as a beacon in today's fast-paced sales environment, teaching us that true success lies in understanding and valuing our customers. From the intricate art of conversation to the transformative power of mindset, *Listen to Sell* is a must-read for anyone serious about elevating their sales journey—an absolute masterpiece in the realm of sales literature."

FARSHAD ASL, bestselling author and leadership expert

"Mike Esterday and Derek Roberts share what to do for real sales success. You must ask relevant questions and then listen—truly listen—to your customers' responses. The authors start with your mindset—what messages you must give yourself for success and how to ensure you have a customer focus. They then introduce you to a logical, sequential sales process that will keep you on track. As a result, you will be a more competent and confident sales professional."

ELAINE BEICH, author of *Skills for Career Success* and *The New Business of Consulting*

"*Listen to Sell* should be required reading for every salesperson on the planet—it gets right to the heart of everything you need to hit home runs. The authors make it clear that success is all about building good relationships and having regular, meaningful conversations. Learn all the sales skills you will ever need in this wonderful book."

JOE SCARLETT, retired chairman of Tractor Supply Company

"Mike Esterday and Derek Roberts nailed it. The new order of selling starts with listening and being truly values driven and customer focused."

KEN TAYLOR, CEO at Training Industry, Inc.

"I have always believed it is attitude, not just aptitude, that differentiates the successful from the less successful. It really is the combo of mindset and skillset that will set you apart. If you nodded 'yes' to that statement but don't know the how-to, grab *Listen to Sell* to learn just that!"

BEV KAYE, coauthor of *Love 'Em or Lose 'Em*

"An insightful and robust read with practical 'Coaching Corners' at every turn to provide sales professionals with the guidance and tools they need to be successful."

HOWARD FARFEL, CEO of TalentSmartEQ

LISTEN TO SELL

How Your Mindset, Skillset, and Human Connections Unlock Sales Performance

Mike Esterday · Derek Roberts

LISTEN *to* SELL

PAGE TWO

Cataloguing in publication information is available from Library and Archives Canada.
ISBN 978-1-77458-489-7 (hardcover)
ISBN 978-1-77458-376-0 (paperback)
ISBN 978-1-77458-377-7 (ebook)

Page Two
pagetwo.com

Edited by James Harbeck
Copyedited by Jenny Govier
Proofread by Alison Strobel
Cover and interior design by Fiona Lee
Indexed by Maura Blain Brown
Printed and bound in Canada by Friesens
Distributed in Canada by Raincoast Books
Distributed in the US and internationally by Macmillan

24 25 26 27 28   5 4 3 2 1

listentosellbook.com

This book is dedicated to the global Integrity Solutions team that works so hard to support clients around the world and fulfill the mission of our founder, Ron Willingham, to "change the way the world sells and serves people."

Contents

Why We Wrote This Book

TOO MANY sales leaders and sales professionals have been misled.

They have been programmed with scripted statements or questions designed to pressure customers into doing something. They talk too much, demonstrate too quickly, and negotiate as if there is only one winner. They've been indoctrinated in a process that's built entirely around persuasion and getting the deal. And they've been told that to be successful, they need to be bolder, more self-assured, and more convincing, even if it feels contrary to their internal values and true selves.

This view of selling keeps a lot of very talented, high-potential people trapped. It's the kind of thinking that gets in the way of real success, which includes job satisfaction as well as material rewards. It's also why we often say sales is the only profession that seems to be consistently defined by those who do it badly.

At its core, selling is about asking smart, relevant, compelling questions to uncover needs that the salesperson can address. But that's only half of the sales equation. Great questions are useless if you are unwilling or unable to truly listen to the answers. This may seem obvious, but the reality is, most salespeople are not great listeners. Fully engaging your ears and brain is a more difficult task than you might think. It takes practice, skill, and will.

It's not easy to be in sales these days. The sales ecosystem is growing more and more complex, with long buying cycles, numerous and unpredictable stakeholders, and a customer base that's both well informed and distracted—and pretty confident they don't need us. What's more, the exponential increase in digital interactions has overloaded us all with enough data and analytics to make the techiest of heads spin.

For too long, those in the sales profession have been shortchanged by wrong-headed notions of what sales success requires and what it looks like. As the selling environment has evolved in recent years, many are beginning to question whether their role still has meaning. Some are wondering whether they even want to be in sales anymore.

This is why we wanted to write a book that celebrates sales as a profession and the salesperson as a respected, valued partner. At Integrity Solutions, after fifty-plus years of working with over 5,000 companies and several million graduates of our programs from 130 countries, we can confidently say that professional salespeople today are needed more than ever. And for the salespeople and sales leaders out there, there have never been more opportunities to be successful and fulfilled in your work.

There is a catch. To be effective, you need new tools, new skills, and more training. Then again, that's always been the case in the ever-changing world of sales. In this book, you'll discover that the secret to sales success lies in mastering the human elements in sales—the universal people principles and behaviors that apply regardless of what is happening in the industry today, last year, or ten years from now.

There are two fundamental factors that make Integrity Solutions a different company and this a different kind of book.

First is our unwavering commitment to a values-based, customer-focused approach to selling. Integrity is in our name on purpose. If you are manipulating your customers—or believe you are—you will limit what you can achieve. But when you build trusted customer relationships grounded in integrity, you will be valued and respected by others and confident and motivated within yourself. This is why we emphasize listening as the essential thread that runs throughout the entire sales relationship. Customer-focused selling requires that we remain present and intent on hearing and understanding what our customers are actually saying. It is how we value them, and it is why we are trusted when offering solutions to meet their needs.

Second is our proprietary methodology for becoming a truly great salesperson. Our research has found that achievement drive, self-belief, and attitude are keys for your selling success. For those of you who feel you've reached a plateau, there are specific actions you can take to get yourself "unstuck." You *will* get beyond whatever roadblocks you are currently facing. This book shows you how.

This book is *not* for you if you're looking for sales gimmicks or some magic formula that quickly turns a hesitating customer into someone ready to sign on the dotted line. Our methods aren't complicated, but they do call for discipline and an open mind.

Most important, they hinge on you. When a product can be ordered online with a click, robots can step in and take care of the sale. But where there are complexities related to the human side of selling, it takes human-focused approaches.

It takes coaching, emotional intelligence, and self-awareness. It takes *you* to make the journey mutually beneficial, fulfilling, and successful.

We wrote this book to lay out our principles of selling better with integrity. We've filled it with examples and insights from our own experience, along with tips, exercises, and assessments. When you use this book to help you learn and grow, you will transform sales into a different kind of experience for your customers—and for yourself.

As we like to say, if someone has a negative view of salespeople, they just haven't met you yet!

MIKE ESTERDAY
DEREK ROBERTS

How to Use This Book

THE BOOK is designed to reach salespeople from a wide selection of roles and responsibilities. While some examples may not be in your industry or type of sales, focus on the universal principles you can apply to specific areas or circumstances that relate to you.

- Read straight through or jump to the chapters you believe will help you most. Keep in mind, however, there is a reason for the way the chapters are ordered. Learn the selling principles first, and then learn how to coach to them.

- The Appendix includes practical resources and tips. Links in the text direct you to free content and assessments that Integrity Solutions offers online.

- The coaching chapters in Part Three, as well as the Coaching Corners at the end of each chapter, are designed for managers but included so that, as a salesperson, you can use the questions and content to be your own coach.

Introduction

"GIVE UP TRYING to contact anyone. No one answers the phone or email anymore."

"The data analytics are wrong... Just let me do my job the way I used to."

"I was doing fine until I was given a different territory."

"If marketing would send better leads, I'd close more business."

"The competition has the same product but at a lower price."

"But I'm not in sales. I'm a customer service rep!"

There are many variables affecting sales success. It can be easy to feel that given the *right* factors—the market, the product, the tools, the data, the competition, a natural sales ability—selling would be easier, and success would be inevitable.

But at some point, when those factors don't line up for you, you get stuck and either plateau or decide to try another company, work for a different division, or consider a career change. Sure, there are tools and analytics that help (or get in the way), but the rewards and confidence that come with knowing you're really, really good at what you do are missing.

You no longer feel in control of your success. You don't feel successful at all.

These are issues that even the most experienced salesperson faces at some point in their career. It's natural for our thoughts to go there when sales has become a process that we're caught up in—and one that's been complicated by massive industry changes. Sales *happen* to us. The market and the economy *happen* to us. Technology *happens* to us.

Then you might ask yourself, What's going on here? Is it the constant barrage of technology, social media, and now artificial intelligence? Would better data analytics, a better CRM, more leads, a great marketing strategy, or a better territory change everything?

No. *The most significant variable in your sales success is you.* This is true when the market is tough. It is also true when times are good.

Let's look at why this is so.

It's a Great Time to Be in Sales

Opportunities to be successful are always present. In the current economy and in today's sales environment—with all the "disruption" that goes with it—the role of the sales professional has never been more purposeful... not in spite of but *because* of what's happened over the past decade.

Anyone who's been in sales for a long time will tell you that it's a numbers game. More contacts lead to more opportunities. Qualifying potential customers with specific needs was always a time- and labor-intensive process. It also was a shot in the dark. Today, however, through analytics and customer data models, organizations can identify potential customers and refine that equation based on specific behavior models, online activity, and demographics. By accurately predicting which individuals are more likely to become customers, you have a much clearer idea of where to focus your efforts. You can also move more quickly and efficiently.

Automation and marketing technology have been transformative in other ways. Sales used to mean getting in a car and spending half the day out on the road and knocking on doors. Maybe you reached two contacts. These days, you can connect, be responsive, and stay in touch by pulling up information on a mobile device. You can automate, sort, and delegate repetitive tasks.

All of the above is good news for salespeople because of what automation and predictive algorithms can deliver. It's also good news because technology augments—even transforms—the role of a salesperson to another level. It puts you in a position where you are ideally suited to be precisely what your customer is looking to find.

These are big shifts, though, and salespeople aren't the only ones facing massive changes. Your customers are in the same boat. They enter the buying process before talking with a salesperson, typically searching online, where they encounter enough choices to bury them in information. As they narrow their search, they are likely guided, directed, fed, or pushed certain information along the way.

This buyers' dilemma puts in play a different kind of algorithm—one that you, as a capable salesperson, help decipher and prioritize. In a world where customers are often more informed than ever, the insights you bring to the sales conversation are more valuable than the most sophisticated algorithms.

Are You for Real?

Trust and authenticity are two of your biggest differentiators.

Buyers crave trust, and yet the gap between what customers believe and what companies tell them has never been greater. Today's customers can tell when they are about to be sold. They sense insincerity, perhaps in how the emails all sound like they've been scripted or how the salesperson starts telling them why they are doing something "all wrong." There are many examples—you can probably think of plenty—and make no mistake: Customers are always tuned in to it. They're thinking, "Does this person truly want to help me, or are they just trying to sell me stuff?"

When customers trust and believe you, they'll not only allow you to get them the right information to make good decisions, but they'll also walk away thinking, "Wow, that was a great experience."

Who Trusts a Salesperson These Days?

LinkedIn research on B2B sales strategies and trends tells us that only 32 percent of people describe sales as a "trustworthy" profession, while 88 percent buy only when they view a salesperson as a "trusted advisor." In analyzing the research, LinkedIn writer Sean Callahan concludes, "Roughly one-third of B2B customers don't trust salespeople and are reluctant to buy from them, let alone listen to a pitch."

Can Someone Speak Human to Me?

There's something else that customers are craving—and you bring it to the table without even thinking about it.

So much of the sales experience has been digitized or commoditized. Customers engage with an interface, a computer, a tablet, an app, or perhaps an online form. They type in a specific word or make a query. Next, they're deluged with pop-up ads, emails, and chatbots coded to sound friendly. In such a sophisticated age of AI, some wonder if the human part of the sales equation is rapidly becoming obsolete.

Just the opposite is true. While there are many situations where customers will value a transactional, non-human buying experience, there are also buying examples where people today are screaming for human connection and interaction. They want to be valued. They want to buy from you, especially when they believe that you have the right intentions, that you are there to help them, and that they can trust you.

None of this can happen unless they know you are truly listening to them—not as a robot but as a human being.

This is the value you bring beyond delivering the greatest new product. When the competition catches up with the same solution at the same price, you still are the salesperson your customers depend on. When they have conversations with you about specific changes in their selling environment, you are the one who can illuminate the situation rather than simply reply with a scripted answer. When they need someone to shift their perspective, you are there to discuss an alternate way forward. When they want someone to validate their fears, you have the courage to face the truth.

Knowledge Alone Isn't All You Need to Sell Well

How are you going to leverage this value into greater sales success?

More than any other factor, you need to think differently. Selling is not pushing a product or making a transaction. *Selling is uncovering needs, meeting needs, and creating value for people.*

According to this definition, sales success isn't the result of a great product or the latest technology. Those help, of course, but they only influence what happens; they don't determine it. Success for a salesperson relies on two factors: skillset and mindset. Skillset, including knowledge and a disciplined process, is always required, especially as the industry undergoes innovations and challenges. But knowing how to sell on its own isn't going to create sales winners. Unless you believe that you have *within you* the mindset for what it's going to take to create value for your customer, all the skills and knowledge in the world aren't enough.

We're not talking about blue-sky thinking or what some might call "toxic positivity." The power of a positive, confident mindset is well researched. The essence of what scientists have uncovered can be found in the book *Mindset: The New Psychology of Success*, by psychologist Carol Dweck. After studying the impact of how conscious and unconscious thoughts affect us and our ability to improve, Dweck concluded that these beliefs "strongly affect what we want and whether we succeed in getting it." In other words, more than any other factor, mindset either makes us successful or prevents us from fulfilling our potential.

The positive news is that mindset is not hard-wired. You choose your mindset. You have the inner power to achieve any goal that you can condition yourself to accept as within your capabilities. You just need to decide . . . and then do the work.

Let's Start Listening to Sell

There are two elements to listening. The first essential element is cultivating a mindset of genuine desire and curiosity to understand. The second is developing the skillset to ask compelling questions and seek thoughtful answers.

When you listen to sell, there are three kinds of conversations you need to master as a salesperson. This book has a section dedicated to each one.

The first is a conversation with yourself: how you talk to yourself about selling—what selling really is, how good you are at it, what matters to you, how good your product is, and how committed you are. We'll show you what we've shown millions of salespeople: how to do the best and be the best by listening to what you are telling yourself.

The second kind is conversations with customers. The best way to get people to listen to you is to listen to them. We have a process for this called AID,Inc.® We'll show you how to use it to listen to the words, body language, tone, and messages in between the lines of what a customer is telling you.

Third are coaching conversations, including listening to effective coaching from your manager. These conversations help salespeople understand themselves and their customers better through a process of questions and thoughtful reflection.

When you put it all together, this book is your guide to developing the mindset and skillset for truly exceptional sales performance. It won't be long before you see the impact, both in how much better you are at meeting customer needs and in how the numbers reflect the change.

We believe in you because *you* control the most significant factors in your sales success. Let's get started on putting that mindset to work.

Coaching Corner

Each of the following chapters in this book ends with a Coaching Corner that is set up to help you think about what you read in the chapter and apply it to your own situation. If you are a manager, the questions and the "power thought" are ideal for using with your team. Salespeople and managers alike, however, can use the Coaching Corner to grow their own understanding of how they approach sales and what they might want to do to take their performance to the next level of success.

Power thought

My good thoughts are powerful;
any negative thoughts are weak.
SERENA WILLIAMS, PROFESSIONAL TENNIS PLAYER

Questions and reflections

Why do you think salespeople succeed or fail?

Beyond product knowledge and sales know-how, what traits most influence sales success?

Most people achieve a level of success they feel they deserve to enjoy. Do you believe you deserve to be performing at a higher level?

Are salespeople even relevant in this new digital world?

If you are a sales manager, do you believe in your people and see possibilities they may not see in themselves? What needs to happen to get your people to sell more?

PART ONE

MINDSET:
CONVERSATIONS
WITH YOURSELF

*Success is more an issue of who
you are than what you know.*

Establishing Purpose

RONA LOVES HER JOB. She is a pharmaceutical sales rep and is very successful at it. However, this wasn't always the case. There was a time when she wanted to quit. She would sit in a physician's waiting room and think, "All of these patients are unhappy with me. After all, I'm the reason their appointment is being delayed."

Rona's mindset shifted the day she visited a horse-riding program where children receiving therapy were being treated with the medication she sold.

She said, "Parents came up and thanked me and told me how the drug brought normalcy back to their children and their families. After that day, everything changed for me. I stopped 'selling pharmaceuticals' and started helping families and kids."

. . . .

YOU MAY have had an experience like Rona's. She was convinced that her only purpose was to sell a product. The experience triggered an emotional reaction—she felt she was a disruptive presence—until she understood the real purpose behind her role as a sales professional.

To be successful in sales, you need to convince people. But, as Rona discovered, the first person you need to convince is yourself. And to do that, you need to know *why* you're selling. The same applies if you are a sales manager who wants to improve the performance of your team. Training can increase skill level. However, you'll likely miss some self-limiting behaviors if you don't address how emotions prevent your salespeople from pursuing new opportunities or completing the activities necessary to advance the sales process.

Emotional Versus Logical

In sales, these *emotional factors* separate high achievers from the rest of the pack.

When Integrity Solutions conducted research on the factors that make a difference in sales performance, 84 percent of sales leaders told us that beliefs (mindset) and values (a general desire to create value for the customer) are at least as important as selling skills and product knowledge. Yet the same research project found that only 26 percent of sales leaders rated their organization as effective at developing such factors in their salespeople!

Understanding how emotions impact sales performance takes work. The conversation starts with defining *purpose*: why you are in sales in the first place. It's why we say selling starts between the ears before it happens between people.

So, it's time to hold up a mirror, take a good look at yourself, ask these questions, and listen to your answers:

- Why am I in sales in the first place?
- How does my purpose shape my actions each day?

You Need a "Get To" Job Instead of a "Have To" Job

Fans of *SpongeBob SquarePants* may remember the rather pessimistic Squidward, who explained to his fry cook, SpongeBob, "In case you've forgotten, here's how things work. I order the food, you cook the food, then the customer gets the food. We do that for forty years, and then we die."

Hopefully, you see the purpose of your job as something beyond this kind of drudgery!

Having a purpose doesn't just sound good. Purpose gives you a better reason for doing what you're doing than just "This is what I have to do," or "This is the way I get paid." Without purpose, whatever job you have makes your life very transactional. We all want belonging, significance, to know that our contribution matters. It's what gives "nobility" to whatever we do.

For a salesperson, a strong purpose spells the difference between being stuck in a job you tolerate or even dislike and breaking through to a job where you achieve more and enjoy what you do every day.

The same applies if you are a manager coaching sales-people. When your sales teams are purpose-driven and sell in a way that aligns with their values, they will consistently connect more successfully with their customers' realities and goals. These salespeople also are more likely to remain engaged in their work. And sell more!

Purpose-Driven Companies

A study of high-growth companies revealed a surprising driver for success: Companies that put purpose at the core of their strategy gained an average compound annual growth rate of 30 percent or more over five years.

The pet supply industry provides a good example. Mars Petcare initially marketed its brand as contributing to overall pet health. However, when it made pet health part of its core business strategy, the company-wide purpose propelled Mars Petcare's expansion into veterinary services—a move that leapfrogged the company ahead of its competition.

Purpose-driven companies aren't just attractive to their customers—they're also magnets for talented people. Successful salespeople want to work where they can make a difference and find meaning in what they do. And when they find that, they stay.

What Motivates You Each Day to Go Out There and Sell?

Purpose gives you the desire—the motivation—to reach your goals. Motivations vary because, well, people vary.

Not everyone is selling a new drug therapy or a heart stent that saves lives. But there can be a greater purpose behind any product or service. Many salespeople, for example, are motivated by the fact that they are selling much more than just brake parts or electrical equipment: They're selling safety, an enhanced work environment, or peace of mind. Others are motivated by the financial freedom that comes from earning a higher income. Now they can give their children a college education at a top-tier school, travel more, or buy a home that accommodates aging parents. You may wish you had additional income in order to make a larger donation to your favorite charity each year. The motivation—the reason—is yours, but when your goals are connected to something that has meaning for you, you're more likely to achieve them.

Achievement Drive

Goals and purpose kick-start another factor: achievement drive. Think of achievement drive as the pure grit you need in order to direct focus and energy to all of your selling activities. Achievement drive works deep in our subconscious, pushing us to do whatever it takes to find creative ways to solve problems, overcome obstacles, and reach our objectives. It's the mother bear in us that won't let anything get in the way of what we know we must do to be successful.

We all have achievement drive; when your purpose, motivation, and goals are clear, your achievement drive is turbocharged. It keeps you going, no matter what, to produce the desired outcomes.

Discovering your purpose takes work and involves deliberately questioning yourself and listening carefully to your responses. Many say their purpose is "making money" or "gaining recognition," but these can be short lived. What's the real reason? Are you working late so you can bring home a bigger paycheck, or are you working late so you can make a meaningful impact? When there is purpose, you are driven to benefit someone beyond yourself. Yes, you benefit from buying that bigger home or giving that extra gift, but the lives of others improve as well.

Purpose has an impact on everything you do. It affects your attitude and how you respond to setbacks. It shifts your entire perspective on why you do what you do. It affects how you prioritize your day and how well you listen. It changes the conversation with yourself and changes how customers respond to your energy and confidence, because confident salespeople gain a lot of credibility from their customers.

If you don't have a purpose, all the great goals in the world won't be enough to help you reach your full potential. *Add purpose, then watch the magic happen.* With purpose, you gain the inner power—the achievement drive—to accomplish your goals. More than knowledge, skills, education, or training, this strong achievement drive is the multiplier of success.

Setting Goals + Purpose = Achievement Drive

(Knowledge + Skills + Education + Training) × Achievement Drive = Success Power

Coaching Corner

Power thought

Don't let anyone tell you that you have to choose between making money and making a difference. Purpose and profit are linked. You can have both. You deserve both. We all do.
LISA EARLE MCLEOD, AUTHOR OF *SELLING WITH NOBLE PURPOSE*

Questions and reflections

What's your story? How did you "end up" in sales?

State a purpose for why you get up each day and go to work. If this is difficult to answer, complete the following: "I have chosen to be in sales because it will make it possible for me/my family/ my customers to... [do what?]"

How do you make the world a better place by what you do? If you had additional income, what could you do to improve the lives of others?

Does selling give you energy or drain your energy? If selling drains your energy, think of reasons why. What would have to change to make a difference?

Internal Beliefs

"**S**AME TRAINING, same tools, same support—why do some salespeople succeed while others fail?"

It's the question that many sales managers and leaders struggle with the most. They have a subset of salespeople who are experienced and well trained and bring a high sense of integrity to their work, but quarter after quarter their sales are average.

Managers scratch their heads looking for an explanation; the salespeople themselves try to understand what the problem is. It's a search for the deeper reasons behind sales success.

And so, we return to the emotional aspects of selling. In addition to knowing your purpose when selling, you need to look at how you perceive yourself and the world around you. What do you believe about yourself? What do you believe about what you're selling? This inner game of beliefs can have a huge impact on your performance.

It starts with your "labels." We all carry them. Lou is "shy," Martin is "headstrong," and Aisha is "good with technology." Most labels were assigned when we were growing up. Over time, these labels became internal self-beliefs or perceptions that you listened to and influenced how you behave. You likely don't realize the impact they are having in your daily life, but if you were told as a child that you weren't good at something, you probably still believe it—whether it's true or not.

Through research and training thousands of salespeople, Integrity Solutions has found that success in sales has more to do with who you are than what you know. That's why it's so important to listen to these conversations you're having with yourself and what they reveal about your self-beliefs. Once you identify these inner beliefs, you can then explore what's influencing them.

Five Influences That Drive Your Sales Success

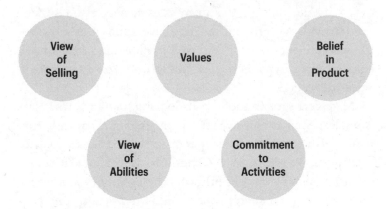

We've found there are five self-beliefs that are most influential for those in sales:

1   View of selling
2   View of abilities
3   Values
4   Commitment to activities
5   Belief in product

We'll go over these beliefs one by one to help you uncover them in yourself or in your team. We'll also explain how negative or incorrect beliefs in these areas influence behavior and what you can do to shift mindsets.

View of Selling

A negative view of selling refers to the stereotype of salespeople we've grown up with in the movies, TV, or just from bad personal experience: someone who talks without taking a breath and is always offering some deal.

Because of this stereotype, many salespeople view selling as an activity that conflicts with their values, especially if they're afraid they'll appear pushy or even dishonest. What's more, many people don't see themselves as salespeople at all. They took a job to provide service and information to customers, and they think selling goes against that mission—that it's profiting at the customer's expense.

For instance, a banker or technical rep may view their role as customer service, not sales (this may even be on their business card). So when their manager directs them to upsell additional products and services to customers, they resist. Even if they are trained in how to ask questions related to needs, they consider these kinds of conversations manipulative and designed just to get someone to buy. They don't view it as customer service.

An incorrect view of selling is equally problematic for those who *do* see their job as selling. Salespeople in industries that require licensing or are highly technical typically consider their role as the expert responsible for educating the client—more like a consultant than a salesperson. The problem is, when you view selling as educating the customer, you'll tend to over-invest in talking and may avoid asking for a commitment. And if your manager insists that you ask customers questions to see if they want additional products, you resist because, after all, you are there to educate, not push a warranty.

Conversely, if you view selling as product-based, you'll talk for hours about the solution instead of using some of the time to build the relationship. In your view, selling is only about the transaction and not about serving customers.

Shifting mindset

A negative or incorrect view of selling influences sales performance for salespeople across all industries and levels. Shifting your mindset starts with how you define selling. Your view of selling is the degree to which you understand and believe sales to be a profession that creates value and helps people. When you view selling as helping create value for people, view yourself as a value-generator, and feel good about the value that your product creates, you look forward to and enjoy selling.

The same principles apply to a non-profit. Most fundraisers don't see their work of acquiring donors and support in the context of a sale. Selling, however, is about identifying and meeting needs, creating value, and building relationships for your organization and your donors—all things that align with the organization's core values and ethics.

Post the following messages somewhere you can see them daily as a reminder of what it means to be a customer-focused, values-driven salesperson:

- Selling is one of the highest callings I can have. It is, in every sense of the word, a noble profession.

- As a salesperson, I make it possible for my customer to do great things by helping them solve a problem. I do so by seeing their situation through their eyes and recommending products and services that are going to be valuable to them.

- As part of my organization's sales team, I am integral to the success of everyone. Someone needs to be the tip of the spear and engage in selling. Otherwise, no one gets paid! That someone is me.

What Does It Mean to "Be in Sales"?

A few years ago, one of our sales consultants spoke to a group of high school students taking a course on entrepreneurship. When he asked how many wanted a career as a salesperson, one lone student raised her hand—and very cautiously. Surprised at the response, our consultant asked what words came to mind when the group heard "salesperson." The same student answered, "trusted, caring, focused on customers." It turned out her parents were both in sales!

Although these future entrepreneurs were considering a career in their own businesses, they couldn't get their heads around "being in sales." It was a stark reminder that our view of being in sales is shaped and reinforced by our experience from an early age.

View of Abilities

Let's say you sell in an industry that targets Fortune 1000 organizations. Until now, you've been selling to front-line managers and doing well. An opportunity comes along where the senior VP of manufacturing is a key stakeholder. Suddenly, there's a million-dollar possibility in front of you. What's going on in your head? What's your comfort level? Do you see yourself as having the confidence or ability to sell at that level, or do you delay making the call?

Your view of abilities is your inner belief about whether you have the necessary talents and skills to be successful in sales. What are your strengths and attributes: Confidence? Experience? A great smile? How smart do you feel: Average? Exceptional? We're talking about those labels again. Over a lifetime, your self-beliefs affect confidence and the ability to be successful. The same applies if you're a manager struggling to motivate a sales team. The bottom line: *Salespeople sell what they sincerely believe is possible for them to sell.*

Most of us are affected by this kind of negative self-talk at one time or another. It's typically called "imposter syndrome"—the inability to recognize our own skills, knowledge, expertise, and achievements. Imposter syndrome causes us to doubt ourselves and even believe that we are a fraud in our work and that it's only a matter of time before we're discovered.

Shifting mindset

Our beliefs are powerful. A negative view of your abilities can become a self-fulfilling prophecy. If you believe you have always been average, that's the way you tend to stay. Even if you consider yourself well above average in some important way, the odds are good that you see yourself as much less able in other areas—which you might excuse by claiming you're just not interested in them. That's how someone who is brilliant in product knowledge can be quietly dedicated to the idea that they will always be terrible at sales.

Skills training, particularly training that focuses on customer conversations (which we will discuss in Chapter 7), helps a lot. Performance management tools will track your productivity and help you set new goals. Training and development alone, however, aren't enough. Whatever your unconscious beliefs, your sales will match them. Tools and techniques only make a difference if salespeople are coached to think differently about their abilities.

The questions presented in the Coaching Corner at the end of this chapter are a good start to shifting your view of your abilities. Later chapters will give you more tools and questions to help shift your mindset about both your view of selling and your view of your abilities.

Values

Successful salespeople believe they demonstrate a high degree of integrity, sincerity, and honesty in all sales interactions. And their values are directly connected with their view of selling. If a salesperson believes that selling means talking someone into something they don't need, their values are going to be conflicted. A similar conflict occurs if they believe the product they are selling might not be the best choice for their customer.

There may be occasions when a sales professional feels their values conflict with those of their sales manager. For example, they may be given a sales script that asks questions that sound manipulative to them, or they are asked to "interrupt" a busy surgeon with a sales presentation, and they know the timing is wrong. When salespeople are asked to do selling activities that go against their values, perceived skills, or sense of right and wrong, it triggers an internal conflict and can decrease their ability to sell.

Shifting mindset

It is important to figure out if your values are being compromised or if other internal beliefs are getting in the way. For example, if you view selling as transactional or product-based, asking probing questions may seem to contradict your inner values. The same applies when a manager pushes salespeople to meet quotas without helping them understand how to sell value beyond the product. The inner conversation the salesperson hears is, "I could never do that!" or "This doesn't feel good!"

But if you view selling as helping customers with their needs, your values will show through—even if that means directing them to a competitor. One of our clients struggled with her view of selling until it finally dawned on her that her role wasn't to go out and sell stuff! "I just need to have conversations with customers to see if they have a need," she realized. "And if they do, it's my obligation to show how I can help them." It was like a light switch turned on.

To be successful, salespeople must answer this question: "Is the way I sell consistent with my inner values?" If your conscious or unconscious answer is "no," you'll perform at a low level, burn out, or quit and do something else. But if you can shift your mindset to see the value you bring as a customer-focused, ethical salesperson, the difference you bring will be rewarded.

When values are tested

What about those times when your values are tested? Maybe you are being asked to do something that conflicts with what you feel is right, like promise something you know the company can't deliver. In these instances, you are correct in pushing back and saying no. Over the long term, however, it is almost impossible to bring your best to an organization that conflicts with your values. There may be good reasons to remain in a sales position for a short term even when you feel your values conflict with those of a manager or the organization. Perhaps the job gives you an excellent opportunity to work at a global company or build your resume in a hot industry, or perhaps the money and benefits are important for your family. Each of us needs to look at our own goals and purpose and decide where to draw the line. If your values are continually in conflict, you will ultimately struggle to be successful anyway.

When considering a position at a new company, identify the values most important to you and ask questions that reveal what the company values. For example: What is the company's definition of selling? How is success measured beyond quotas?

Commitment to Activities

Your commitment to activities is how diligent you are about doing the activities that long-term sales success demands. It's not enough to understand which activities are necessary for success; you must be willing to do them.

When salespeople feel confident and look forward to their everyday role, they welcome doing results-producing activities. But when salespeople dread certain aspects of their job, they consciously or unconsciously choose the least threatening tasks. Some are aware they are avoiding what they should be doing, like making follow-up calls and new contacts. Others don't realize they are focusing on all the wrong things. They put activities off or do tension-relieving busywork, like sorting out their call reports. It occupies their time but isn't impactful.

Shifting mindset

Commitment to activities may not actually be a belief. It is more of a symptom that one or more of your view of selling, your view of your abilities, your values, and your belief in the product are in conflict. The question to ask is, *Why* are you avoiding doing what you know is going to help you sell more successfully? Here are some common reasons:

- If you think that selling is "bothering people" or interrupting their day, you'll avoid sales conversations and opt instead to say, "If you need something, let me know."

- If you are uncomfortable asking for the sale, you'll talk too much instead of initiating an action step.

- If you don't believe you have the ability or experience to talk with high-level executives, you'll resist making that contact and talk instead with someone in the organization with whom you're already comfortable.

- If you question the product's value, you'll resort to transactional or product-focused selling instead of activities that draw out the value and need.

- If you believe you are being asked to do activities that conflict with your values or integrity, you'll avoid them and do something different to feel productive.

Uncovering these roadblocks can be a challenge. In Chapter 14, you'll find some effective coaching questions to ask yourself or your salespeople. If you can address what's getting in the way, the discipline and motivation to do more impactful activities will follow. If you recognize yourself in one of the examples above, it's time to listen more closely to what's happening. To be a successful salesperson, you need to understand what activities are necessary for success and be willing to do them... even the tough ones you don't want to do.

Belief in Product

Your belief in product is how passionate you are about the products and services you're selling and the value they create for customers. Belief in product is another area that can conflict with values, specifically when the salesperson believes the product they are demonstrating is inferior in some way or costs more than that of a competitor. Belief in product can be a challenge, particularly when there are few, if any, additional product differentiators.

Shifting mindset

Sales success is who you are, not what you sell. It's easy to increase product knowledge, but selling is a customer-focused activity.

Your role as a salesperson is to listen and use knowledge, insight, and attentiveness to help customers make the decision that's right for them. This is value you bring in addition to the product's value or your ability to recite features. Strong indicators of value include making your customer's decision process more effective, respecting and adapting to the way your customer communicates, and being honest when a solution is not right for what they need and telling them so. (In Chapter 5, we'll introduce a sales process for helping match customer needs to product benefits and value.)

The benefits and cost of a product may be suitable for some customers but not others. Or the value may be beyond the product itself—maybe the parts and service are available locally, or you can offer direct support by monitoring delivery or providing training, for instance.

There's another factor at stake when salespeople don't understand or believe in the value delivered. They silently communicate their hesitation through behavior and attitudes.

Customers intuitively pick up on the lack of conviction and passion, so they buy from someone else. The salesperson's confidence drops, so managers push harder. It's a vicious circle.

The reverse is true when salespeople understand that the product is only part of what they deliver. The full equation includes the company that stands behind the product and the difference customers experience when they engage with you as the salesperson. That positive experience feeds your confidence and energy. Customers respond, and you sell more.

Where Is the Value?

A piece of plywood is a piece of plywood. How would you sell the difference if the price and quality were the same? You can't—if there is product parity and a limited understanding of value. But value can be assessed in various ways, depending on the customer and their needs.

We strongly believe that organizations and products create value for customers. We also understand that different things are valuable for different people and purposes. If you're selling high-quality wood that costs more, the value is that it lasts longer. If you're selling inexpensive wood that won't last as long, the value is that it saves money for people who only need it for a short time—a longer lifespan just isn't valuable to them.

We will discuss tips and coaching ideas related to belief in product in Chapter 8 when we explore the Demonstrate step of AID,Inc.

Shifting Mindset Is a Lightbulb Moment

Your self-beliefs affect the value you bring, which affects how you feel about your own role. When you deliver value that is important for your customers, you will meet your sales goals—an achievement that undoubtedly is one sign that you're successful in sales. But more than that, you will gain confidence from believing in yourself. You will be secure in knowing that you have what it takes to deal with whatever challenges or setbacks come your way and know what to do to move forward.

Many salespeople we talk to want more meaning in their lives. A whole new awakening takes place when your mindset becomes "I'm doing something for people."

The next chapter looks deeper into what's happening between the five dimensions that can make a big difference in your commitment to activities and how to pull these influencers into alignment.

Coaching Corner

Power thought

Salespeople are the most important people in any organization. Until a salesperson gets an order, nobody in the company has a job.
CHRIS GARDNER, AUTHOR OF *THE PURSUIT OF HAPPYNESS*

Questions and reflections
What was your view of selling growing up? How does this shape your view of selling today?

What aspects of selling make you uncomfortable? What needs to happen for sales to feel like a noble profession for you?

Turn to the Appendix and read through the Integrity Selling Values and Ethics. Select statements that reflect your own beliefs. Name three or four values you believe are essential to you, and describe how you live those values in your work.

Have you ever worked for a manager whose values were not in sync with your own? If so, how long did you last in the job? How do you currently feel about that decision to quit?

What do you personally offer customers beyond the product? (Think of the times you've helped in the decision-making process or responded when there was a problem with delivery, implementation, or service, for example.)

Sales managers may want to focus on helping sales teams sell what might be considered a mediocre product. Encourage your salespeople to return to their customer profiles and review their circumstances.

- Do they need a product with all the advanced options, or does the basic model fit their current needs?

- Which customers are looking for this type of product? Why does it meet their needs?

- Which customers need to be directed to a more innovative or high-quality product, and why?

What activities keep you busy through the week? Which are impactful in terms of getting business? Building relationships?

What activities do you avoid, even dread? Do you know why this happens? (For example, perhaps you've had several customers who have a negative view of selling, and that experience is affecting how you approach other customers.)

3

Getting in Sync

H AVE YOU EVER tried to focus on a distant object with a pair of binoculars? The binoculars are a pair of telescopes mounted side by side, each supplying an image to one eye. But you don't see two images. You see one unified picture. For this magic to happen, the two telescopes must be parallel to each other. They need to be in alignment.

Now imagine if there were five lenses to get in sync!

Chapter 2 looked at the five internal self-beliefs commonly found in sales. They are depicted in the graphic to follow as separate lenses through which you view selling, abilities, values, commitment to activities, and belief in product. The light circles represent each of the five areas of self-belief and the dark circle shows all five in alignment.

Ideally, the five views should be aligned. A clear, focused mindset makes it possible to perform at your best. But if you are struggling in one or more areas, the lenses pull apart and your vision is blurred. Depending on the size of the gap, this misalignment can lead to self-doubt, inner conflict, disengagement, resistance, or outright discouragement. Salespeople and their managers see the impact of such negative outcomes every day: Activity levels drop, performance suffers, and achievement drive slows down.

All of this is why, several decades ago, Integrity Solutions set out to find a way to bring the five lenses into alignment. The result is our Sales Congruence Model™.

Sales Congruence Model: Five Lenses to Align!

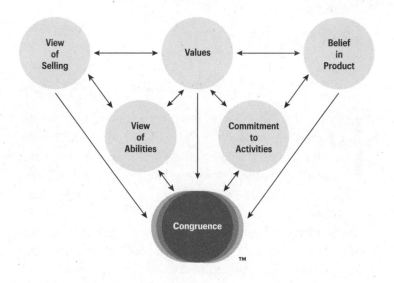

Getting Familiar with the Sales Congruence Model

The Sales Congruence Model is designed to help salespeople listen to and recognize how their internal beliefs affect their overall performance and then take steps, through skills and mindset, to pull their beliefs into alignment.

- **First step:** Learn how the model works.

- **Second step:** Identify your gaps or weaknesses.

- **Third step:** Work toward getting—and keeping—all five areas aligned or "in sync."

Learn to "Work" the Sales Congruence Model

Bringing these self-beliefs into congruence takes work! For example, you may not believe a product will deliver value to your customer. This will need to be resolved by adding more product knowledge or understanding the value for certain customers. Look at the model and how each belief affects the other, and think about your strengths and weaknesses in each area.

- Gaps or imbalance between areas can cause mental and emotional blocks, which inhibit sales success. (This is often the case when your values or belief in product conflicts with your view of selling or of your abilities.)

- The wider the gap, the more likely you will experience internal stress and feel stuck.

- Bringing beliefs into congruence is powerful because it releases achievement drive.

Making the Sales Congruence Model Work for You

One of our Integrity Solutions trainers likes to say, "When one or more dimensions are out of alignment, it's like driving a car with the brakes on." So, how do you replace these emotional blockers with enablers?

The five dimensions in the Sales Congruence Model can only come together when positive actions, attitudes, and values are practiced in everyday selling activities. Before you can shift your mindset to overcome a belief or use it to your advantage, you have to identify where a belief comes from.

Each of the following examples describes a typical congruence gap and how you—ideally, with the coaching of your sales manager—can overcome the gap.

View of selling

You love doing product demos and building confidence with your product knowledge, but you avoid asking needs-focused questions for fear your customers might reject what you're selling.

Gap: You believe in the product. That's good! But there's a gap in your belief in selling, which limits the kinds of customers you are comfortable with.

To gain congruence: Skill training in how to ask better needs-focused questions will help, in addition to a mindset shift. If you are a manager, communicate to your salespeople that they have excellent product knowledge, but role-play questions to help start a conversation and keep it going. Help them see the value they are creating for customers and assure them they have the potential to perform at a higher level.

View of abilities

You have a positive view of selling and excellent product knowledge, but you lack confidence in your ability to bring value to an executive-level conversation.

Gap: Senior-level audiences have different demands and expectations than many salespeople are used to dealing with, and your self-limiting beliefs are getting in the way of being successful selling to this level of audience.

To gain congruence: Build new skills to address the unique expectations and demands of C-suite customers. You also need to develop the necessary mindset to call on senior executives. They have problems you can solve, just like anyone else.

Values

You know a particular product has been plagued with major issues that have frustrated your customers. This challenges your values as an honest, trustworthy advisor to your customers. As a result, you avoid activities related to upselling the product or linking its features with benefits during a product demonstration.

Gap: You have high values but low belief in product.

To gain congruence: You need to find ways of stressing the benefits of buying from a company that stands behind its products because of its high corporate values. In this way, you can protect your clients and still emphasize the product's value. As a manager, provide client success stories and other validation, and praise the rep's high ethical standards.

Commitment to activities

You are passionate and knowledgeable about your core products. However, you find yourself too busy to discuss new products and opportunities your company has introduced.

Gap: There's always a reason why a salesperson avoids activities necessary to make a sale. We often mistake being busy with being productive—doing tension-relieving versus results-producing activities. Perhaps you doubt your ability to sell something new or you don't believe the new product is valuable for your customer.

To gain congruence: Ask yourself, Do I understand the necessary activities and expectations? How can I restructure my time and conversations? Am I willing to try something new? Also, review the other four beliefs to see what is in the way of doing the necessary activities.

Belief in product

You have a positive view of selling, high values, and belief in your abilities. But when the product you are selling is available from the competition at the same price, you have trouble believing that you are delivering any additional value.

Gap: Your belief in product (and the value delivered) is conflicting with the value you bring as a sales professional.

To gain congruence: The ability to create emotional bonds with your customers is the true x-factor that drives customer loyalty. Shift your mindset to believe that beyond product and price, it is you who can create deep, trust-based relationships, which makes you and your company stand apart from the rest. As a manager, help your salespeople see the value and benefits they offer and help with needs-based questions that uncover these benefits.

Do an Alignment Test

Congruence gaps can cause conflict and stress, and they're often the root cause of stifled productivity. An alignment check ensures smooth running for the remainder of the year. In sales terms, this involves assessing whether your knowledge, skills, and values are sufficiently congruent to release the motivation and achievement drive necessary to reach your unlimited sales potential.

Look back over the year so far to see if you can detect any patterns. What's been particularly effective? Where are you getting the best return on your energy, effort, and time? Where do you keep hitting a wall? Are there certain activities you're avoiding? Is there something else you could be doing that would add more value?

If you're the sales manager, these and other alignment checks should be part of your ongoing performance strategies:

- If the year has been going slow so far, you may need to discuss a salesperson's view of their abilities. A negative view can become self-perpetuating, putting the person at risk of falling further behind.

- If the processes are in place but people aren't following them, there may be a lack of commitment to the activities necessary to achieve quota. As you review progress toward goals, focus on the degree to which the person is engaging in the activities and where there might be gaps. Together, you may discover some quick remedies that will make the salesperson more efficient and help accelerate the sales cycle.

You Are the Most Significant Factor, and Awareness Is the First Step

In recent years, those in service roles, such as customer service reps, have been asked to upsell and cross-sell additional new products to their clients. This can be threatening to those who don't consider themselves salespeople. Introducing a new credit card or an additional checking account may feel manipulative, the very opposite of serving. The principled nature of the Sales Congruence Model is particularly appealing to this group. It helps reposition their mind to see that "selling is serving, serving is selling; I can do this, and it's the right thing to do."

For others, gaining congruence removes many common emotional barriers, such as fear of rejection and call reluctance, that prevent salespeople from selling up to their actual

capabilities. The barriers are replaced by achievement drive—
the energy that helps you reach your goals. Instead of feeling
stuck, you want to do results-producing activities. As you
develop internal zest, confidence, and a deep feeling that
what you're doing is right, you'll be unconsciously freed up
to sell on higher levels.

Using the Sales Congruence Model is a way to help you
think about these factors. Ignore them or pay attention to
them: The choice is yours.

Those self-beliefs influencing your success are "will"
issues, not "skill" issues, and that's one of the most important messages in this book: *You are the biggest factor in bringing
about your success*—not some external force like the economy, which sales enablement platform your company uses,
or where you went to school. Combine this awareness with
your purpose, your positive values, and the skills provided
in the rest of this book, and then look out sales world, here
you come!

Now it's just a matter of choices. Choosing how you sell to
customers and connect with customers leads us to the next
Listen to Sell conversation: *conversations with customers*.

When you view selling as creating value for
people, when you are confident in your abilities,
and when you feel good about the product,
you do results-producing activities.

You ask good questions because this is an
activity that aligns with your belief in helping
customers buy a product that's right for them,
and not one they've been "talked into."

When you follow up with a decision-maker,
you do so confidently, not fearing rejection.

As a result, you become one of those
high-performing salespeople with internal
zest, confidence, and a deep feeling
that what you're doing is right.

You work harder, smarter, and longer,
and in turn you sell at higher and higher levels.

Coaching Corner

Power thought

I'm not the next Usain Bolt or Michael Phelps.
I'm the first Simone Biles.
SIMONE BILES, OLYMPIC GOLD MEDALIST

Questions and reflections

What labels have created self-beliefs that limit your impact? What steps might you take to break through a limiting belief boundary affecting your sales success?

You may not be able to change your thoughts immediately, but awareness is an essential first step. Make a list and rate yourself in the five self-belief areas discussed in this chapter. If you have a couple of loyal customers, ask them to rate you or your salesperson from their point of view. Now you can see what might be getting in your way and how you can change these obstructions to enablers.

Use the Sales Congruence Model as a coaching tool for yourself or, if you are a sales manager, with your salespeople. The Sales Congruence Model assessment tool we present in Chapter 16 is a resource you can use to identify and address gaps.

PART TWO

SKILLSET:
CONVERSATIONS WITH CUSTOMERS

Selling, at its heart, is not about talking people into something they don't want. Selling is about finding the people who can benefit from what you have and making it easy for them to buy.

4

Communicating Human to Human

ONE OF THE memorable characters in the 1993 movie *Groundhog Day* is the annoying insurance salesperson, Ned Ryerson. In Ned's words, "Whenever I see an opportunity now, I charge it like a bull. Ned the Bull. That's me now."

Ned claims he's an old school chum of the main character, Phil Connors (played by Bill Murray). It's clear that Phil has no interest in talking to Ned about life insurance, but Ned never takes the hint. He walks alongside Phil, and on every repeat of the day he pesters Phil with a different pitch, each as annoying as the previous. Eventually, Phil snaps and punches Ned in the face. When the movie played in theaters, the crowd would always cheer at that part.

All the best intentions and achievement drive in the world aren't going to bring success if salespeople fail to listen to and connect with their customers, or if, like Ned, they connect badly! Buyers recognize the hard sell from a mile away. Even if the approach is less "salesy," customers don't have time or patience for an information dump or a generic product pitch based on some general assumptions.

Engagement with customers is more important than ever in an age of chatbots and artificial intelligence. A scripted, one-size-fits-all approach isn't going to do the job. With a positive sales mindset in place—strong purpose and aligned values, beliefs, and attitudes—success in sales ultimately comes down to the *conversations with customers*.

Today's Buyers Want Help

As we explained in the introduction, technology has forced massive changes on both salespeople and their buyers.

Salespeople struggle today because customers look for buying channels, not sales partners. One report puts the preference for a B2B purchase free of human interaction as high as 43 percent.

Anyone who can connect to the internet can fully educate themselves about what they need—or believe they need—without engaging with a human being. Online ordering and who-knows-what's-next artificial intelligence give customers all the reasons they need to extract themselves from a buying process that involves a salesperson—which is exactly what is happening. And it's leaving sales leaders shaking their heads and wondering how to reach actual buyers.

Buyers struggle too, because unless they are purchasing commodities, the buying process has become increasingly complex. There are countless options and solutions to consider; new products and services emerge almost daily. Plus, purchasing power often resides with not just one person but multiple stakeholders, each with different priorities and motives.

As one researcher on the subject reports, "The single biggest challenge of selling today is not selling, it is actually our customers' struggle to buy."

Customer challenges fall into one of two categories:

- They have a need or gap to fill, and they've identified that need. But they don't need an order-taker to fill the gap or some plug-and-play solution. They need someone to help them navigate through the questions, data, and decisions necessary to confidently make the right choice.

- They don't know what they don't know. They need someone to sit down, listen to them, and help them think through the problem their organization is trying to solve and what the ideal state looks like. In many instances, this includes helping them prioritize what's important to them and perhaps change their perspective and come up with ideas they wouldn't have considered on their own.

Buyers need conversations. But they need conversations that help them *buy*, not help the salesperson sell. Recent Gartner research highlights the challenge for today's buyers, noting that "buyers value suppliers that make it easier for them to navigate the purchase process."

The same research found that customers were 2.8 times more likely to experience a high degree of purchase ease and 3.0 times more likely to make a larger purchase with less regret when they believed they had received helpful information from salespeople that advanced their decisions.

Human Conversations with Human Customers

The customer challenges described above create the ideal opportunity for salespeople who can have better-quality *human* conversations with their customers—conversations that customers recognize as more valuable and different from the competitors. This is true now more than ever, given that many conversations are virtual and time is such a priority.

Integrity Solutions works with a number of contact centers that record hundreds of phrases into an automated response system to help agents identify needs. The challenge is when agents rely solely on these systems instead of truly listening to needs and the meaning behind the words. Digital automation is here to stay, but there is an essential role for a real person who can listen and bring creative, engaging insights that make one company's products stand out as different from another's.

The quality and content of the conversations you have with customers will be among the determining factors in whether you'll meet your sales goals this year. A foundational element of your training and coaching should be about working on these conversations. Mastering these conversations requires that you become acutely tuned in to the humans in the equation—you and your customers—and how different personalities affect the success of those conversations.

The Behavior Styles® Model

Selling is an interactive experience. We know that the need to be understood is one of the strongest human needs. A conversation adapted to your customer's preferred style of interacting shows them you're really listening to them and allows you to connect more quickly and build trust. When prospects unconsciously trust, they feel at ease with the salesperson and are more likely to buy.

The four Behavior Styles are shown here, along with their guiding motivations.

Behavior Styles Model

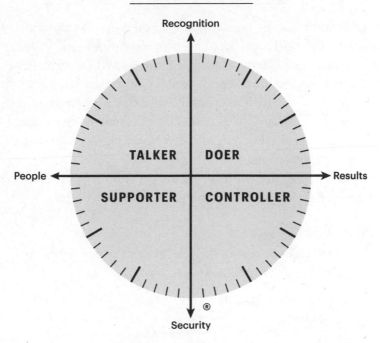

Most people are combinations of two or more styles, and there are degrees in which styles are expressed. Use the Behavior Styles analysis that follows as a tool to guide your approach, but don't consider these fixed categories in which you can just slot people. Also keep in mind, there are no "good" or "bad" styles, just different people—and, therefore, different conversations. (We've also provided a Behavior Styles Checklist in the Appendix.)

Recognizing Behavior Styles Through Observation

Observant salespeople will pick up on clues to customers' concerns and be prepared to provide the understanding, support, or reassurance they need. Talkers and Doers exhibit high energy, while Supporters and Controllers have lower energy. Some, like Talkers and Supporters, are more influenced by emotion. Doers and Controllers are more rational. Recognizing these tendencies can have a significant impact on your sales success.

The following examples give insights into how to identify different styles of customers and connect with them.

The Talker

Expect to hear: "Great to see you. How's the family? Let me introduce you to my colleagues..."

- Outgoing and friendly
- Values personal relationships
- Decides based on emotions and facts
- Not as interested in the details

Talkers are affable, friendly, and social. They want you to like them and show interest in them, their activities, and their families. They'll be easy to approach, and they make decisions emotionally.

Talkers are motivated by people and recognition—they're all about relationships and social value.

Conversations with Talkers: Let them do most of the talking to begin with, but keep them on task and moving toward a workable solution. Your biggest challenge to success will be getting them to focus. They like to talk about a lot of different topics, and you could spend too much time building rapport.

Look for a transition point, perhaps something you have in common, in order to bring up the purpose of your meeting. Then outline the reason you're there and what you'd like to discuss or learn about.

The Doer

Expect to hear: "We booked the call for thirty minutes, so let's get to it. What do we need to discuss today?"

- Direct, forceful, and results-oriented
- Requires concise, focused information
- Makes quick decisions
- Has clear objectives to achieve

Doers show high energy, confidence, and authority. They typically come across as demanding, but that's because they are fearless decision-makers. They know what they want and will do what it takes to get where they want to go. Expect fast, focused action once they've made up their minds.

Doers are motivated by recognition and results—they're all about high standards and performance.

Conversations with Doers: Demonstrate that you respect their time and goals by being prepared to meet their needs quickly. Rapport with Doers often happens at the end of the call, so get them talking to you at the start with a pointed, results-focused question.

They dislike chitchat, so it's a bad sign if you're doing all the talking. They'll typically shut down quickly and look to wrap up the conversation if you ask too many questions— they believe you should research ahead of the call. In presentations, Doers prefer concise information like bullet points and checklists. Don't get them bogged down in details.

The Controller

Expect to hear: "What studies or proof can you show me?"

- Detail-oriented, deliberate, and organized
- Relies on facts, evidence, and data
- Weighs all options before deciding
- Lower manifestation of energy and emotion

Controllers are logical, no-nonsense people who value accuracy, efficiency, and organization. They want you to listen and thoroughly understand them. They might appear overly critical, but that's just because they like to assess and study from all angles. They rely on evidence to make decisions, so they want facts, data, and proof points. They're going to weigh all the options and read everything you give them. Silence is okay. This gives them time to analyze.

Controllers are motivated by results and logic—they're all about being thorough and sticking to the facts.

Conversations with Controllers: It may be challenging to build a relationship with a Controller since they aren't as open as other styles. It's best to get their thoughts on a specific topic. Be prepared, and bring something they can validate and engage with—and have evidence to support your claims.

When presenting, be thorough, provide documentation, and use fact-based communications. Validate the potential success of a solution by providing a rationale for how and why it will work. Focus on benefits and the resulting return on investment (time, money, energy, etc.) from *their* perspective.

The Supporter

Expect to hear: "We've always had positive results with our current product. But we're hoping you can leave us with some reports to review and a reference."

- Needs time to process information
- Likes to establish trusting relationships
- Reluctant to change current buying habits
- Laid-back and friendly

You'll like Supporters immediately. They are down-to-earth and approachable, and they expect the same from you. Make sure you establish credibility and build their trust before offering a solution. Just because they are easy to talk with doesn't mean they are committed to buying. They need assurance that they've covered all the risks first.

Supporters are motivated by security and trust. They're about getting things done through hard work and patient perseverance.

Conversations with Supporters: Build rapport based on relationships. That goes a long way with a Supporter. Try beginning the discussion by connecting personally: "I know we have a lot to get through today, but—before we get started—didn't your daughter have a soccer tournament? How did it go?"

Because Supporters don't want to hurt people's feelings, it can be hard for them to voice contrary opinions. Help them by allowing time for questions and encouraging participation to gain consensus. They dislike pressure of any kind, so offer a plan for what would happen if your proposal didn't work out for them.

Behavior Styles and Buyers' Persona Profiles

Buyer personas, also known as ideal customer types, are research-based profiles prepared by marketers. They are invaluable for prospecting, defining business priorities, and setting sales targets. But they are only tools. Behavior Styles are a more intimate way to understand your customers when you try to interact with or influence them.

As a salesperson, you work near or on the front line. You are typically the first one who hears a customer concern and can respond to it. You are the one who can pivot when the conversation changes or a new challenge is revealed. Behavior Styles give you a way to see beyond the persona and to listen and gain the kinds of insights that make every conversation with your customer impactful. Being able to recognize an individual's style will help you uncover information about them and their challenges, such as these:

- What are the significant factors that affect how well they do their job?

- How is their performance affected if they don't have the proper equipment or it repeatedly breaks down?

- To whom are they accountable, and what must that person accomplish?

- What happened two weeks ago that will change their work environment for the next six months?

- What is "value" to them?

- What wastes their time?

Understanding Behavior Styles can help you gain deeper insight into each customer's unique motivation and desired outcome.

Understand Behavior Styles, Change Your Selling Culture

An understanding of Behavior Styles can result in a culture-wide change in sales organizations. Consider an established, global company facing new competitors and product parity across its brands. The only way to stay ahead is to move away from being a transactional seller of products to building stronger relationships with customers.

Building such relationships begins with recognizing Behavior Styles. This allows a company to deepen its understanding of customers and what's unique to them. Now the company has a whole new way of serving its customers. The company pivots from product seller to problem solver—a culture change that keeps them at the top of their industry.

Customers Have a Right to Buy the Way They Want to Buy

Behavior Styles are a reminder that customers have the right to buy the way they want to buy.

Too many salespeople fail to understand this truth. They become frustrated when the customer keeps asking for more data or won't decide. Or they start piling on features if they think the customer is hesitating or losing interest.

That brings us to another side of the model to consider. Each of us brings our own behavior style to our work, which means as salespeople, we sell to others the way we would like someone to sell to us. If you are detail-oriented by nature, you are comfortable with the customer who keeps asking for more data. If details drag you down, you may frustrate customers by rushing through a technical part of the conversation.

Better conversations start with identifying your behavior style, identifying the customer's behavior style, and then adapting your conversations for each unique sales encounter. As you learn to adapt your conversations to make the customer feel more at ease, the relationship will improve, and you'll close more sales.

There are as many different conversations with customers as there are customers. And every customer and salesperson who is part of these conversations comes with their own personality and behavior style.

We'll give more examples in the next three chapters to help you recognize Behavior Styles and apply what you've learned in your customer conversations.

First, let's look at the sales process that is going to guide those conversations.

Coaching Corner

Power thought

If you want to interact effectively with me,
to influence me ... you first need to understand me.
STEPHEN R. COVEY, AUTHOR OF *THE 7 HABITS*
OF HIGHLY EFFECTIVE PEOPLE

Questions and reflections

Look at the four Behavior Styles described in this chapter. Which two are most like you? Turn to the Appendix or scan the QR code below for our Behavior Styles Checklist.

Now think of your customers. Can you start to identify their Behavior Styles?

- What clues help you recognize a customer's style?

- Which style is easiest for you to sell to? Which one is the most challenging?

- How would you adapt a call for each of the four styles?

Coaching managers may want to look at each team member:

- Identify their style and tendencies.

- Develop a list of best practices for communicating with each style.

5

The AID, Inc.
Sales Process

R EADY, SET, TALK! In most instances, salespeople today
have a few minutes, even seconds, once they finally get
through to a customer, and they need to get that conversation started. Gone are the days when you could
lead with a rehearsed pitch or depend on friendly chitchat
while you gathered your thoughts. The physician is standing
in the doorway, checking her watch, and asking, "What have
you got for me today?"

Given the limited time available for capturing a customer's attention and the importance of making a connection,
you don't want to leave the conversation to chance. Every
salesperson, regardless of experience and expertise, requires
a disciplined process. Having a process allows you the freedom to be present and the confidence to say, "I don't have to
manufacture the conversation. I know where I want it to go
and how to move it in that direction."

There are many sales processes available. The good ones
are built around how people engage with one another, from
first impressions to a trusted relationship. Integrity Solutions

has developed a sales process that for over fifty years has given salespeople a framework for an organized sales conversation of any length, whether you have two minutes or two hours. We call it AID,Inc.

Six Simple Steps to Better Sales Conversations

AID,Inc. is organized into six steps:

1 **Approach:** Establish rapport and break the barriers of preoccupation.

2 **Interview:** Identify needs, challenges, and problems.

3 **Demonstrate:** Show how your products and services fill identified needs.

4 **Validate:** Prove your claims and heighten trust. (The acronym AID,Inc. borrows the "I" in val-i-date.)

5 **Negotiate:** Understand and work through problems and concerns.

6 **Close:** Ask for an appropriate commitment to action.

These steps cover a communication process for every interaction you'll ever have with every prospect, lead, and customer. If the process sounds straightforward, it is. This is one of the reasons AID,Inc. has been so successful. It can be applied to a short conversation sale or a long, complex sales cycle, which institutions like hospitals, banks, and utilities go through before making a purchase decision.

Practicing AID,Inc. reinforces the importance of having a customer-focused mindset. It is designed to help you listen, understand, and uncover needs, not just execute a transaction.

Values and integrity aren't just implied. They are your rules of engagement, integrated into every step and conversation.

A Timeless Truth

In 1980, Integrity Solutions' founder, Ron Willingham, observed how a skilled salesperson sold him insurance. Instead of convincing Ron to make a purchase, the salesperson guided him through the buying process, identifying what he needed or didn't need and helping him decide one way or another.

The experience led Ron to redefine selling and create the AID,Inc. sales process, grounded in principles of integrity and values. The principles are timeless because human nature has not changed, regardless of what has changed in the world and the sales industry.

As one of our sales facilitators likes to say, "AID,Inc. is just a very human way to have a conversation."

No Step Left Behind

There are a few application principles to be aware of when using AID,Inc.

First, AID,Inc. is the opposite of the "show up and throw up" mentality. Each step is essential and gives salespeople a road map to the sale. It makes sense: With a structured framework, you mentally know where you're at and what you need to do before you can get to the next step.

You can expand or compress the steps depending on the circumstances, but there's no skipping. The steps are designed to work whether you have five minutes in the hallway selling pharmaceuticals at a doctor's office, thirty minutes in a virtual meeting, or two hours in a conference room with the top executives at the largest company in the state. Do your research, ask questions, and find a problem that needs to be solved for your customer. All of this leads to a higher level of competency. When salespeople apply it and see it working and fitting together, they start to have confidence in their ability. They become committed to the greater purpose of serving and selling.

It's About Time

Second, the guidelines for *time spent talking* versus *time spent listening* matter.

Listening well is part of a customer-focused mindset that demonstrates values of respect, empathy, and patience. Beginning at step one, you have a chance to differentiate yourself from your competitors by simply using your ears more than your mouth.

The following chart shows how this works. Each bar represents a step in the AID,Inc. sales process. The width of each bar represents the relative amount of time spent on that step. The darker shaded area at the bottom of each bar represents the approximate amount of time you should spend talking in that step, while the lighter area at the top represents the amount of time you should spend listening.

The AID,Inc. Sales Conversation Model

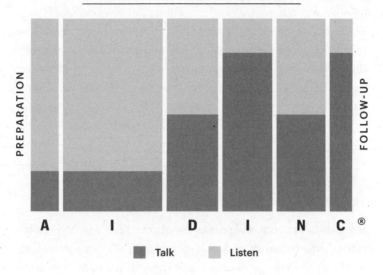

PREPARATION

FOLLOW-UP

A   I   D   I   N   C ®

■ Talk   ▨ Listen

Using AID,Inc. in a Call Continuum

Finally, AID,Inc. adapts well when there are multiple meetings with various decision-makers and team members:

- The Approach and Interview steps might occur several times, as multiple stakeholders and technical experts are invited to be part of the process.

- The same applies to the Validate and Negotiate steps, which deal with different concerns depending on each buying group and what they see as risk factors.

- The Close step might take place over weeks, with one Close being a decision to meet again before the final decision to purchase.

Using AID,Inc. for this kind of call continuum provides flow between meetings and a connection between each step. There is a structure and a record of what took place and where the process is headed next. What was promised or committed to at a previous meeting can be carried forward to the next. The process comes across as organized and efficient—and so do you.

A Common Language Across Territories and Countries

Many organizations have cross-functional teams acting in silos rather than together as a cohesive, mutually supported unit. In one study we conducted, less than 19 percent of companies said their salespeople consistently follow an established sales process. When teams lack a common way of interacting with customers, it can impact continuity, trust, and loyalty.

By introducing a straightforward sales process like AID,Inc., companies are able to establish a common language and culture for their teams. As a result, they can compare issues at various steps in the sales process, share experiences, and improve performance across the organization. Finally, everyone speaks the same language!

Using AID,Inc. for Non-Salespeople

If you are a health care clinical specialist, technician, bank teller, HR professional, or physician, you most likely don't consider yourself in sales. Make no mistake: You *are* in sales.

You are interacting with potential customers and influencers to explore values, understand needs, gain trust, answer questions, and explore ways you can provide support. Support could be providing data to help with a business decision or providing expert advice on current regulations or compliance issues.

When our team at Integrity Solutions introduces AID,Inc. to "non-salespeople," we emphasize that AID,Inc. is much more than a sales tool. It is a process for having conversations that build relationships and establish credibility, from Approach (building rapport) to Close (how we can partner together).

Putting AID,Inc. Into Practice

Key points to remember about AID,Inc.:

- AID,Inc. is not just another sales process. It's a framework for having an organized sales conversation.

- It may not be possible to complete each step during one engagement, particularly with a complex sale. AID,Inc. can take place in one engagement, but it also can stretch out over weeks or even months.

- Don't skip the Approach or Interview step, even if you already know your customer. There should always be a point of reconnection, especially when new stakeholders or sales team members join the discussion.

- AID,Inc. is a flexible system. It can be expanded or compressed like an accordion, depending on the call circumstances. And it's not always linear. There may be times when you go back to a previous step to clarify needs.

- Closing is about asking for the appropriate commitment that keeps the call continuum moving forward. It may be about asking for the business, or it may be about simply confirming the next appropriate step. A negative response is proof that one or more of the five previous steps in AID,Inc. wasn't properly completed.

Confidence

There's a final by-product of AID,Inc.: It delivers incredible confidence. By using the process as a framework for conversations, you have a game plan at the beginning of every sales engagement. You can stop the conversation and see where you are, go back if needed, or know where you're going next time. At a time when business is fast paced and so much is unexpected, the stability of a tried-and-true process is invaluable.

The next chapters take you through the steps in AID,Inc. so you can see how to put it into practice, depending on the nature of the sales situation. Each step addresses how to adapt the process to different Behavior Styles and buying motives. As you adapt your conversation, you signal that you're listening, that you appreciate and respect the customer for who they are, and that you're committed to helping them reach the best decision for *them*.

Coaching Corner

Power thought

The way you treat people, what you say and do that affects them emotionally, is more important in bringing out the best in people than all the education, intelligence, or experience you might have at doing your job.
BRIAN TRACY, SPEAKER AND AUTHOR OF *EAT THAT FROG!*

Questions and reflections

In many industries, it is easy to become very product focused. Practicing AID,Inc. reinforces the importance of a customer-focused mindset.

Look at the time allocated to listening in the first two steps. Does this surprise you? How might this change the way you engage with customers?

Which element of AID,Inc. do you think you do best?

Which elements are the most challenging for you?

What is one area in which you'd like to strengthen your skills?

6

Approaching to Establish Rapport

LUIS WORKS FOR inside sales at an insurance company. He makes phone calls and answers inbound calls selling casualty insurance. He knows, however, that selling over the phone has its limitations. Despite the lack of visual cues, Luis quickly builds rapport with his customers and gets them to share what is truly important to them. For example, a customer recently called to simply add a teenage driver to his insurance policy. Because of the intentional way Luis began the conversation and focused on getting to know the caller, the customer opened up more about his family. As a result, Luis was able to do more than just add the teenager. He helped the customer understand his increasing risk profile and was able to mitigate that risk with a new umbrella policy. He ended the call with a very grateful customer.

．．．．．．．．．．．．．．．．

WHETHER WE like it or not, people pick and choose who they talk to. In a cold call, a follow-up on a lead, or a face-to-face over video, the Approach step in AID,Inc. is all about getting customers to speak with you about themselves and building trust and rapport. Starting at the Approach, you need to be listening so you can quickly determine what kind of person this is, what their behavior style is, and how you can be relevant and appeal to the way they want to be spoken to so you can have an effective conversation.

Goals of the Approach Step

- Break the barriers of preoccupation.
- Demonstrate a sincere interest in your customer.
- Establish rapport.
- Listen.

Break the Barriers of Preoccupation

Think about the last time you felt like someone was *really* listening to you—for example, when the other person took in every word you said without interrupting when you paused or reflected.

In today's incredibly distracted world, showing others that you are present, engaged, and interested is increasingly important. Salespeople who can "tune out to tune in" have a true advantage. You will be clear and focused in your thinking, and customers will see immediately why you stand out from your competitors.

Breaking the barriers of preoccupation starts with being well prepared. (We discuss preparation in detail in Chapters 12 and 13.) Preparation includes taking a few minutes ahead of each call to calm your mind and visualize a positive encounter. Maybe you had a flat tire on your way to work or you dropped your mobile phone in the toilet. If you can't get these events out of your mind, delay the call.

Tune Out to Tune In

The Approach step suggests that you listen 80 percent of the time. This means being totally "tuned in" to your customer—aware of their tone of voice, body language, and what is being said. And that means tuning out everything else.

Listening can be a challenge for the best of us. It's human nature to focus on ourselves. Doing so feels good in our brain, which means we need to make a conscious effort to stop and listen!

Listening is a skill to be applied throughout AID,Inc., but it is critical during the Approach. If customers don't think you're listening to them at this stage, they might not listen to you at all.

Show a Sincere Interest in Your Customer

Failure in the Approach step is likely a failure to prepare well. Preparation is the best way to demonstrate that you are interested in learning about a customer and finding out (instead of assuming) whether they need or want what you are selling.

There are no substitutes for the kind of pre-call research and planning we recommend ahead of the Approach. You want to know as much as possible about the business or organization, the customer, and how they like to buy (their behavior style). Chapter 12 takes you through this. The tips in Chapter 13 are designed to equip you from the very beginning to ask smart questions and stand apart from other salespeople.

Establish Rapport

Human beings establish rapport by connecting with shared interests and understanding. Draw the customer into a conversation about something that creates connection.

Be curious. Be attentive. The most effective way to *get* someone to talk is to *let* them talk. Science confirms this. When people talk about themselves, they feel good because it activates regions in their brains associated with pleasure, motivation, and reward. When you respond by listening intently, they feel valued.

Listen

During the Approach step, remain customer-focused, not product-focused. This can only happen if you show sincere interest as you listen and connect with them as a person— not just as an opportunity for a sale. You want to hear what they are telling you because you care about delivering value to them and making sure they make the right decisions.

Like Luis did in our example, listen for a significant comment. Tell yourself, "I am valuable in this conversation, and I'm genuinely interested in this person. I'm here because they need me, or I'm here because I'm going to discover that they don't need me. Only by listening can this happen."

Approaching in Less-Than-Ideal Circumstances

Even when time is limited, the way you handle the Approach signals your intent to understand the customer before you ask them to consider your product.

Try a simple acknowledgment: "I realize you may not be expecting this conversation, and I'm sure there are lots of others trying to tell you about their business. However, I'd really like to get to know you and understand your business to see where we can provide value."

The same applies if you approach using email. Avoid a predictable question such as, "What keeps you up at night?" Begin your message with a question or information that's relevant to your customer. Say something to show you have already made a sincere effort to understand their business or learned from something they said earlier in the conversation.

Complex sales take multiple Approach steps. During a long sales cycle, it's not enough to have a strong relationship with one senior executive. To forge genuine relationships with multiple stakeholders, you must return to the Approach step several times throughout the buying process. When you do so, link previous conversations with the current meeting so everyone can be at the same step in the process.

Adapting to Behavior Styles

Behavior Styles play a significant role in AID,Inc., beginning with your Approach. If you know your customer's style, you can plan accordingly. If the contact is a referral, you can ask the person who referred you about the person's behavior style. If neither of these is an option, begin assessing their behavior style while you listen so you can adapt as you continue.

Certain signs can give you clues:

* You'll find it easy to gain rapport with Talkers. They'll be open to a friendly conversation that builds the relationship. They'll also want to include others in the conversation. Talkers use phrases that include others, like, "We're not sure how we feel about this idea." The challenge is to keep them on task.

- Doers want to get to the point. They want to socialize less. Keep them focused by sharing the goals for your call as soon as possible. The challenge here is that Doers may ask for the feature specifications right away. Resist, but acknowledge the request.

- Don't be surprised if a Controller doesn't acknowledge you when you enter the room. They need facts and logical proof. It's likely they're already doing research and weighing their options. The challenge is that they value accuracy, efficiency, and organization, so be well prepared.

- Supporters may refer to the company they have "always done business with." This is because they are loyal and reluctant to change. But they are patient and will engage in the sales process with you. The challenge is it will take time to build their trust. Don't be too quick in assuming they are committed to a solution.

- There's a quick way to uncover someone's behavior style: Look for the energy level. Talkers and Doers have high energy; you can hear it in their voices and see it in arm gestures. Controllers and Supporters are more reserved and have lower energy. Observe their body language when you can, and note the lower-pitched, neutral, and soft-spoken tone of voice.

Once you identify Behavior Styles, you can start adapting your questions. As new stakeholders are introduced to the process, refer to notes you've prepared about their role and behavior style.

Your own behavior style

Don't forget the impact of your personal behavior style during the Approach. The biggest conflicts typically happen between Talkers and Controllers and between Doers and Supporters. Being aware helps you adapt the way you enter the conversation.

- Talkers jump in with casual, friendly conversation. A customer with a Controller style might show visible disinterest until you get to the more detailed and relevant information that appeals to their analytical way of thinking.

- Doers want to move through the sales process efficiently and may find it a challenge to be patient, while Supporters hesitate or need more time.

Turn On That Camera!

Breaking the barriers of preoccupation can be a real challenge when connecting virtually, especially if participants don't turn on their video. When setting up the meeting, let participants know your camera will be turned on. Invite everyone to do the same. See our Virtual Meeting Tips in the Appendix for more about how to have effective virtual meetings.

Be Relevant

Sales has always been about making a positive first impression. And it happens fast. You may have about seven seconds (and some psychologists say it's more like one-tenth of a second) to make the desired impression on a new customer or prospect. Having an impact also requires relevancy. You may come across as smart, well informed, experienced, even charming, but during the Approach, does the customer see a business reason to keep talking with you? Do you still have an opportunity-related reason to keep talking to them? When this is the case, conversation will move smoothly into the next step, the Interview.

Coaching Corner

Power thought

The old aphorisms are basically sound.
First impressions are lasting.
JESSIE REDMON FAUSET, EDITOR AND WRITER

Questions and reflections

What natural abilities do you bring to the Approach that build trust and engagement with your customers?

How do you get focused ahead of a call so your mind stops thinking about a hundred different to-dos?

How do you make a positive first impression during a cold call? When meeting on a virtual platform?

Think of a few of your current customers. What kind of Approach works with each one's behavior style?

7

Interviewing to Identify Needs, Challenges, and Goals

STEFAN, WHO SELLS for a global manufacturing business, is falling behind in meeting quota and advancing his sales. His colleagues are all doing fine, and he can't understand why they are succeeding and he is not. Stefan's manager sits in on some of his calls, and she hears him ask what she describes as predictable information-gathering questions.

With his manager's help, Stefan changes the way he prepares for his calls. He crafts questions like, "If you made the adjustments you just suggested, how would things be better?" This kind of high-impact question shows that he is genuinely interested in listening and understanding their needs. He proves that he's more than just a vendor with a price list; he's a partner who understands the motivation, the drivers, and the urgency in his customer's world. As a result, his sales improve dramatically.

. . . .

THE INTERVIEW STEP is the heart of AID,Inc. It sets the stage for everything that happens—or doesn't happen—next. It all comes down to the questions you ask.

Goals of the Interview Step

- Further put the customer at ease.

- Help the customer discover, clarify, and verbalize specific wants or needs or further any dialogue from a previous conversation.

- Prove you've listened by helping to prioritize what they need.

- Uncover the following:

  - **People involved:** others involved in the decision

  - **Buying criteria:** specifications or requirements

  - **Decision process:** steps and timing for a decision

Knowing the Kinds of Questions to Ask

As a customer-focused salesperson, you need to find a way to encourage your customer to have a conversation with you about their challenges and needs. A conversation won't happen if you immediately jump in with a solution. It happens when customers realize through your questions and body language that you genuinely want to listen to what they have to say and expand your understanding.

Open-ended questions, for instance, contain words such as *who, what, where, why, when,* and *how.* Because these questions can't be answered with "yes" or "no," they are more likely to create a conversation you can continue to direct with your response.

Compare these questions:

Not-so-smart question: Can I show you why our new product line is considered the best?

Answer: No.

Result: Conversation shuts down.

Versus:

Open-ended question: How do you manage logistics at your different warehouses?

Answer: The customer gives an overview of how complicated it is when there are different truck size and weight laws.

Result: Customer talks, salesperson listens.

Once you have a response, use follow-up questions for additional insights. Follow-up questions start with prompts like, "Tell me more…." "Please explain…." and "How do you track this information?" *Now* you have a conversation.

Good Questions Versus Great Questions

Good questions send a message of competence; great questions cause your customer to stop and think, "Hey, this isn't an ordinary salesperson!" They send the message that you're someone who can bring clarity to people's thinking and decision-making processes.

Great questions are what we refer to as high-impact questions. The GAP Model™ can be used to guide these kinds of questions. It is designed to help customers recognize what is missing—the gap—between their current and desired situations.

There are four areas to ask about when using the GAP Model.

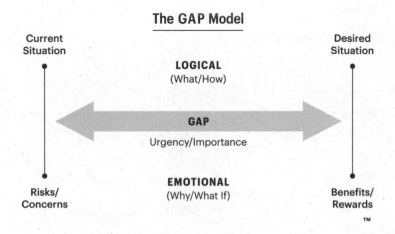

The GAP Model

Current Situation

Desired Situation

LOGICAL
(What/How)

GAP
Urgency/Importance

EMOTIONAL
(Why/What If)

Risks/ Concerns

Benefits/ Rewards

™

The first two are questions most salespeople ask. They are "what" and "how" questions, which provide a factual picture of what is happening today in the organization and clarify the customer's goals and outcomes:

Current situation: Tell me about the products or services you use and how satisfied you are with them.

Desired situation: Tell me about the goals and outcomes you want to accomplish but are not experiencing.

The second two are questions most salespeople *don't* ask. They are "why" and "what if" questions that draw out fears and negative outcomes as well as motivations and rewards:

Risks and concerns: What might happen if you stay in the current situation?

Benefits and rewards: Tell me about the outcomes you might enjoy if you make a change.

In most cases, a gap will emerge between where someone is and their desired state. The bigger the gap, the greater the opportunity.

Getting Customer Buy-In

Your job as a salesperson is to provide a suitable solution in the next step of the AID,Inc. process, Demonstrate. Risk/ concern and benefit/reward questions require more ownership of the answer. The gap the customer describes is the one *they* believe is important to fill. Therefore, the motivation to find a suitable answer is theirs.

This is where understanding the model becomes very powerful. Answers from the top half of the GAP Model are *informational*, but answers from the bottom half are *motivational*. Given that most people make sales decisions based on emotion, you can see why it's important to move to the second two types of questions. The logical ("what?") nature of the current- and desired-situation questions requires less commitment from the person being interviewed. They can simply answer these questions without revealing whether they think the information is important or not. However, questions from the bottom half ("why?") evoke some kind of evaluation or a qualified response. The person being interviewed is being asked to provide insight, prioritize thoughts, reveal a concern, describe an impact, or articulate a reason for action.

When a customer takes ownership of a thought or need in this way, they are much more open and motivated to find a solution that fills the gap.

Applying the GAP Model

When using the model, ask the customer to describe the *current situation*. The current situation will be an honest assessment of what's lacking or creating a challenge—for example, increased competition, loss of productivity, delivery issues, or customer loyalty.

Next, ask about the *desired situation*. These will be objectives related to what is missing in the current situation—for example, achieve a greater market share, reduce downtime, streamline logistics, or increase customer satisfaction.

Now, ask about the *risks and concerns* involved with staying in the current situation. Your question could be something like, "What, if anything, concerns you about continuing in your current situation?" Finally, explore *benefits and rewards* if they made a change. This could be organizational impact or personal benefits, such as achieving credibility, career aspirations, or peace of mind. Listen and clarify if there is a sense of urgency by asking how important it is that they close the gap.

Other questions could include the following (see the GAP Analysis Questions in the Appendix for more):

- What (or who) is driving...?
- How impactful is...?
- What is the significance of...?
- What is the motivation for...?
- How important is...?
- How does [this] compare to [that]?

- How has the organization prepared for...?
- How would you prioritize...?

Note that it may not be possible or necessary to ask questions from every area. If you have a call continuum, for instance, there will be an opportunity to ask questions from other areas.

As you listen to your customer, begin to sort out what they are telling you. Paraphrase all points back to them to demonstrate your understanding. Finally, take the information you now have and ask questions about urgency. Follow up with questions to help the client prioritize their dominant wants or needs or to get agreement.

How significant is the movement for them? Is this something they need to do now? In other words, is it a strategic priority? Or is the timing not quite right? These are straightforward questions, but they are critical to ask at this stage because they affect the overall decision moving forward. There's never a need to pressure people. Customers will often put pressure on themselves once they discover a gap between where they are now and where they'd like to be.

Using the Model in Different Ways

Sometimes, as in the example with Stefan, you have time to prepare before you use the model. Take the time to research the current and desired situations so you can move sooner into questions about risks and concerns and about benefits and rewards.

Other times, you won't have this luxury. You move from Approach into Interview and need to pick up clues from their current situation in order to bridge to a question that gets to the heart of their motivation or urgency for a solution. You'll also discover that a few strong questions from the bottom half of the GAP Model can actually fill in quite a few blanks from the top half.

Pause for Silence

Be patient. When you allow your customer more than a few seconds to think about and respond to your question, you will have a better chance of getting your desired response. Silence may indicate the customer is thinking about an appropriate answer. Be okay with awkward pauses. If you jump in, you might miss an important opportunity.

Adapting to Behavior Styles

You can learn skills that help you conduct better Interviews. These skills can help you ask the right kinds of questions and move the conversation forward. However, every customer brings distinct motives and needs to a conversation. Knowing how to apply Behavior Styles makes it possible to adapt your questions to how each unique customer prefers to communicate.

Watch for signs that help you ask better questions or redirect a conversation from going off the rails. If you've misread the behavior, be ready to adjust. You can tell by the customer's voice that they are losing interest, for instance, which means you may be moving the conversation along too quickly.

- Doers may get frustrated if you keep trying to pull more "what" details out of them. Get them to talk about results, what they are trying to accomplish, and the consequences if they don't address what's getting in their way.

- Talkers will be easier to move to the "why" questions, but expect lots of discussion and ideas. You'll need to pin them down on priorities and timelines.

- Controllers expect that you've done a full analysis of their current situation before you meet, so don't waste their time. They've likely also done their own risk and reward analysis. Move them to the bottom of the GAP Model. They'll see the urgency if loss of productivity or return on investment is at stake.

- Supporters might get stuck at the top of the GAP Model because these conversations make them more comfortable. They will be influenced by factors that put brand reputation and customer loyalty at risk. Raise these as risks, but be patient as they process the information.

One of the best ways to improve your Interview is to write questions before the call and review them based on your customer's behavior style (assuming you know it). Questions should target specific needs and challenges and build upon previous discussions.

- List your perception of wants, needs, or problems that your products or services can fill.

- Identify specific types of information that will help you better understand needs, concerns, or problems.

- Prepare! (We cover this in detail in Chapter 12.)

Applying Mindset

Getting off to the right start during an Interview begins with the mindset you bring. When your view of selling is that you are there to help, customers sense your confidence, feel at ease, and are willing to talk.

Thinking back to our discussion of the view of selling in Chapter 2, you'll recall that "selling" can be viewed in two different ways: either as manipulative—"I want to ask you questions that will lead you and set you up for what I want to sell"—or as sincere and unbiased—"I want to ask questions to understand if you have needs I can help you meet."

Your own behavior style

Part of preparation includes reviewing your own behavior style. What tendencies influence the way you approach conversations? After working with thousands of clients, we have found that although Talkers and Doers are most common, salespeople with any one of the four styles can be successful.

- Many successful salespeople have a Supporter behavior style. Supporters are good listeners and excellent at showing patience when customers have a lot of questions or need more time to consult with colleagues or do additional research.

- Talkers are good conversationalists, which makes them naturally effective during the Interview. But they need to remind themselves of the importance of listening when they do so.

- The same applies to Doers, who must sometimes put aside their need for efficiency to make time for feedback.

- Controllers don't need a reminder to prepare, as preparation is part of who they are! However, a salesperson with a Controller behavior style needs to be careful not to over-prepare. At some point, you need to reach out and make the call.

Our research into why salespeople succeed or not tells us that when sellers are hesitant to ask for a commitment later in the sales process, it's usually the result of a poor Interview. Give your Interview step the time it needs before moving to the next step, Demonstrate.

Coaching Corner

Power thought

Nobody is more persuasive than a good listener.
DALE CARNEGIE, AUTHOR OF *HOW TO WIN FRIENDS AND INFLUENCE PEOPLE*

Questions and reflections
Ninety-three percent of communication effectiveness is tone of voice and body language.

- How do you use your voice and body language on a telephone or video call?

- How do you make the Interview effective when communicating by email?

What is the difference between listening to understand and listening to respond? (This is an excellent question for managers to ask salespeople.)

How does your behavior style influence your ability to listen?

What questions have you asked in sales conversations that resulted in additional insights or information about

- risks or concerns;
- benefits or rewards;
- urgency or importance;
- buying criteria; and
- the people involved in the decision process?

8

Demonstrating Your Solutions

JON SELLS FOR an electrical distributor. His products include everything from large wire spools to wall switches. His typical sales process has consisted of getting a bid for a job and then quoting the components requested by the contractor for that given project.

However, during a recent project with a church that was installing a new sound and lighting system, he failed to gain any traction on the project. After the call, he thought about how it went. "I realized that I was fixated only on the Demonstrate step, and I was doing it in the wrong way," he said. "I was so intent on getting the technical aspects of the job that I failed to listen to what was motivating their need for the new system in the first place."

As a result, Jon began to connect the solutions he Demonstrated directly with what he learned in his Interviews. He took time to drill down in a discovery session, asking questions about what the customer wanted to accomplish, what elements were most significant to them, and how they might create the ideal experience.

By doing so, Jon was able to uncover needs the client hadn't thought of before. This not only improved the quality of his interactions, but it actually increased the scope of his quotes and changed him from vendor to partner.

The tendency to jump to "show and tell" too soon is a common mistake. It happens once a salesperson like Jon believes the Interview step is behind them. It also can happen when customers hesitate because there is something on their minds that's getting in the way of hearing what you have to say.

. . . .

THE DEMONSTRATE STEP in AID,Inc. is when you translate the needs you identified in the Interview into a solution. But you can only effectively position your product if you remember that a customer-focused Demonstration should be a dialogue. Yes, you are "showing" at this step and keeping your customer engaged. But the ideal dialogue also requires active listening and asking for feedback—even if it's feedback you'd rather not hear.

Goals of the Demonstrate Step

- Identify specific needs from the Interview and repeat them to confirm you've heard them and understand the customer's dominant challenges.

- Link product features and benefits to customer needs.

- Adapt the Demonstration to fit the behavior style of each decision-maker.

- Use feedback questions to make the Demonstration a dialogue.

This Should Slow You Down

To slow down so you can focus on what's being said and how to continue the conversation, break the Demonstrate step into four tasks: repeat, show, translate, and ask.

Repeat their needs: First, take time to confirm what you've understood from the Interview. Your statement might be, "As we agreed, your objective is to increase your delivery of finished goods by 10 percent while finding efficiencies. Overall, this should decrease expenses. Is that correct?"

If they don't agree, either make an adjustment or go back to the Interview process to see what has changed.

Show and translate benefits into value: You can show the product and demonstrate how its benefits translate into value for the customer. But here's the challenge. Everyone defines value differently. Rarely is price alone the primary determinant of value; instead, it's included in a mix of several factors. The value might be tangible, psychological, or social, or it might fill other unique needs.

Ask for feedback: You want to know your customer's reactions, feelings, and opinions at this stage. This part of the interaction proves your genuine desire to fill your customer's needs. Most important, it gets both of you involved in helping them make the best decisions.

When there is more than one stakeholder, the Demonstrate step must account for the motives, goals, and interests of all those influencing the decision. Let everyone have a say. What does each influencer have at stake, and what are the risks and rewards of not deciding?

By addressing both the needs and concerns of each stakeholder, your Demonstration should naturally move you through to the Validate and Negotiate steps. If it doesn't, you'll need to return to the Interview to bring everyone on board.

Don't Let the Customer Take You Down the Show-and-Tell Lane

Even when a customer asks for one, a product-focused Demonstration can be overwhelming for them. In some instances, it can even come across as condescending. If your customer insists that you focus on the product, turn the conversation into a dialogue with these tips:

- Keep calm and sell value. Instead of talking about the product, follow the process above: repeat, show, translate, ask.

- Repeat back to them the acknowledgment, need, or problem.

- Explain the product feature that fills the need or solves the problem.

- Summarize with the corresponding customer benefits.

- Above all, give your customers space to think something through, instead of correcting or out-talking them.

Adapting to Behavior Styles

How are you going to Demonstrate value according to behavior style? *You don't have to translate every single feature.* Pick the ones that address dominant needs uncovered in the Interview.

Ask yourself, What motivates this customer or each decision-maker at this meeting? Different stakeholders within an organization perceive value according to their individual roles and Behavior Styles. For some, the equipment or an upgrade relates to benefits such as pricing, technical specifications, or repair and maintenance. For others, new equipment affects customer care or may reduce waiting time. To engage with every stakeholder and address value effectively, figure out which features provide the benefits that are most important to each buying group.

Are they looking to increase efficiencies? Be greener? Save more lives? Become the number-one choice in their sector? If you sell through another vendor, remember your customers' customers: What's motivating them?

- Talkers like to think of you as a friend who cares about them. Highlight how they'll look to others and enjoy owning your product. Ask about the rewards of positive reviews. Above all, guide the conversation so it stays focused.

- Doers need to be slowed down. Talk about results, the bottom line, and the achievement. And keep your presentation short and the meeting efficient. Assure them you'll take care of the details and deliver results.

- Controllers want to know you've taken their need for data and evidence seriously. They'll show little emotion and give less (if any) feedback compared to Talkers or Doers. Prepare for abrupt questions. They'll be more critical in evaluating your presentation, perhaps by demanding proof or evidence to support your claims.

- Supporters aren't likely to see value in a new product on the market unless you provide a safe course for them to proceed. Don't be afraid to ask them about their fears. Listen and acknowledge what they are telling you. Let them know you understand the risks and you're not going to pressure them.

Your own behavior style

Your own behavior style also affects what you highlight as value. When meeting customer needs, you'll want to temper your own bias with what your customer needs to hear.

- Controllers and Doers naturally want to talk about quantitative demonstrations of value—for example, data, evidence, and research.

- Conversely, Supporters and Talkers look for more subjective demonstrations—for example, customer experience, relationships, and testimonials.

What Is Value?

Recent research from Bain & Company shows that business customers bring more subjective, even personal, concerns to the buying process when defining value.

To uncover customer priorities regarding value, Bain analyzed scores of quantitative and qualitative customer studies conducted by the firm over three decades. The goal was to examine what mattered most to B2B buyers.

The research uncovered five categories of value: table stakes (price, compliance, etc.), functional, ease of doing business, individual, and inspirational.

Let Your Client Drive the Decision—Not You!

Imagine if your customers were comic book characters with thought bubbles over their heads. What would they be thinking? Keep this in mind when you Demonstrate. You want to make space for the customer's opinions and feedback. Give them time. Be willing to listen to negative thoughts and hesitation.

You build loyalty by giving customers what they want. The best way to do this is to ask feedback questions, such as these:

- How does this sound to you?
- How can you see this working for you?
- Are there concerns we haven't covered?

Once the Demonstrate step is complete, you'll be pleased with your progress. You have begun to confirm what they need and are building trust with your customer. Validation of that trust, and working through concerns and objections, will continue through the next steps.

Coaching Corner

Power thought

Just having satisfied customers isn't good enough anymore... if you want a booming business, you have to go beyond satisfied customers and create Raving Fans.
KEN BLANCHARD AND SHELDON BOWLES,
AUTHORS OF *RAVING FANS!*

Questions and reflections

The work you've done on your view of abilities and belief in product makes a big difference during the Demonstrate step. You're committed to a customer-focused rather than a product-focused transaction. You've already thought about how the product can bring value to unique customer needs.

As you consider effective ways to Demonstrate your products and services to fill customers' needs, think of this process:

- Which features match specific customer needs?

- What are the benefits of each feature?

- How can I present these benefits differently to each behavior style?

When you apply this thought process to specific customers, you will deliver a laser-focused, customized Demonstration and improve your ability to close more business.

9

Validating So People Believe Your Claims

AS JEN MOVED THROUGH the steps in AID,Inc., she sensed her customer was showing reluctance to make a decision about the product she was selling. An ethical and confident salesperson, Jen knew she needed to Validate her own fears as well as provide Validation of the product and company.

It turned out the customer was overly concerned about risk. In this case, Jen was able to provide assurance the customer needed about the company's reputation for quality and customer service. She wasn't afraid to ask her customers what they were really thinking. Her questions weren't tied to a selling situation. They were simply a way of making sure the customer's needs were being met and value was created.

By doing so, she built a reputation for truly listening and promising to provide the understanding, support, and reassurance customers need.

. . . .

JEN'S APPROACH is what the Validate step is all about—throughout the entire sales process. It's placed here, in the middle of AID,Inc., for a reason. If you haven't developed trust and belief, the Negotiate and Close steps probably won't drive a decision. Or you'll get a decision, but it won't stick.

Keeping promises, acting with integrity, and treating people with mutual respect is just the right way of doing business. It shows in your behavior when there is genuine desire to create value and, in turn, your customers intuitively feel your sincerity. Validation then extends beyond what you bring as a salesperson. It is part of what customers go through when they choose your company to do business with. They know they won't be let down by the products, and at a broader level, they view your brand as one that stands for high ethics and principles.

Goals of the Validate Step

- Present yourself as a trusted advisor.

- Establish yourself as a different kind of salesperson, defined by who you are as a person with high ethical standards.

- Successfully answer three questions that are in your customers' minds:
  - Can I believe and trust you?
  - Can I have confidence in the value of your product or service?
  - Can I be assured that your organization will stand behind what it sells?

Building Trust

You can't force Validation when it comes to what others think of you. Selling is the beginning of a relationship, and nothing is going to begin—or last—without trust. You build trust with your customers starting with first impressions in the Approach and continuing through the entire buyer/seller relationship.

As customers get to know you, they build confidence and trust in you, your products and services, and your organization.

Although Validation happens throughout the entire buyer/ seller relationship, we put it in as the step ahead of Negotiate and Close because it answers the question, "Does the potential customer trust us and believe our claims?" In other words, if trust and confidence are missing, the chances for a sale aren't great.

Validation When It Comes to You

Let's start with you and the relationships you build by acting with integrity and ethical sales principles. Being someone your customers can trust is a surefire way to Validate yourself. Trust is a reflection of who you are, the values you bring, and the honesty you demonstrate through the process. It doesn't happen instantly, and it is not a one-time act. When people see values-driven behaviors in you, they intuitively feel your sincerity, and you can achieve a very high form of Validation.

There's no better way to create trust than through a relationship built on connection, authenticity, respect, and integrity. When you look at the Approach, Interview, and Demonstrate steps, consider how these trust factors can be applied at each step.

Connection: Customers want to know, "Why are you contacting me?" Beginning at Approach, you have an opportunity to come across differently from your competitors. You do so through the interest you show in your customers and the questions you ask. Establishing a connection in this way positions you as a value-generator rather than someone who is product-focused.

Authenticity: There's a saying, "Be yourself. Everyone else is already taken." We've talked in earlier chapters about how salespeople are portrayed as pushy and insincere. Salespeople with the healthiest and highest self-esteem don't have overblown egos. They are highly successful sales professionals who view their job as creating value for customers. Authenticity is demonstrated when customers can tell through your words and actions that you are there for them, not there to sell to them.

Respect: Respect is earned when you listen and make time to understand the customer and their business. You earn their respect during the Demonstrate step when you show your product knowledge, provide proof of evidence, and successfully link benefits to value. You even show respect when you acknowledge that you don't have the right solution for them right now.

Respect also is demonstrated when you accommodate the Behavior Styles of your customers in your conversations. Feeling valued and understood is a fundamental human need. Imagine how you come across to a customer when they can see that you "get them."

Integrity: Integrity shines through all your conversations when you do the right thing for people because it's the right thing to do. This includes being willing to be truthful about the advantages and potential limitations of your solution. This is in contrast to customer expectations that salespeople over-hype the positives. When you gain this kind of customer belief in your integrity, you have achieved the highest form of Validation. You'll reap the rewards in terms of customer loyalty and repeat business.

Mindset and Validation

Salespeople who demonstrate integrity in everything they do often take for granted what their sense of values and ethics means to their customers. When preparing for a call, take a moment to consider the value you bring to every interaction:

- I am capable.

- I have the product knowledge and listening skills to present the benefits to my customer.

- I am going into this meeting to help my customer make the best decision.

- I have values I stand by. My customers trust me to do the right thing.

Validating Your Products and Company

Banners on a website that read "Professional," "Respect," and "Client First" promote admirable qualities, but what do customers need to experience that turns these words into something meaningful?

Customers need confidence that they can trust the products you sell. But in addition to quality and dependability, they are looking for transparency, honesty, and accountability in how the organization does business. Such high ethical standards are increasingly viewed as a priority, and for good reasons. Publicly traded companies that were designated the World's Most Ethical Companies in Ethisphere's Ethics Index outperformed a comparable index of large-cap companies by 7.1 percentage points over five calendar years.

Throughout the AID,Inc. process, there are various opportunities to Validate the products you are selling, the company, and the brand you represent. For example, the company likely posts its policies on corporate social responsibility, sustainability, and diversity. Research products such as Gartner's Critical Capabilities and Magic Quadrant reports evaluate vendors. Other survey organizations may rate the company in terms of how it treats employees. Your firm may also have Validation resources, such as case studies, testimonials, product comparison charts, and webinars.

Adapting to Behavior Styles

Different Behavior Styles, of course, are searching for different types of Validation:

- Talkers are influenced by what others think. Provide testimonials and referrals. Infographics catch their attention (a necessity when Talkers are involved) and are easy for them to share with others.

- Once Doers trust you, they make decisions quickly. They'll also decide not to trust you right away, so the Approach step is crucial. They like to make comparisons before they decide. A checklist that compares the product as well as the brand makes it easier for a Doer to see the differences at a glance.

- Controllers want to see evidence. Case studies and vendor reports in their market space that show quantitative results are a good idea. They are most likely to look for proof that a company's actions are aligned with its overall statement of corporate responsibility.

- Supporters are seeking trust at every step. They get things done by establishing credibility and trust. Be thorough and transparent. They want to know you, but they also want to know what your company represents.

Validate Beyond the "Mission and Values" Statement

A company's brand on the outside is only as good as its brand on the inside. Customers can quickly tell if there are gaps or mismatches between what a company states on its website and how it does business and engages in the world.

As a salesperson, you are a direct extension of your brand. Your actions and motives in regard to ethics and integrity further Validate your products and company with current and future customers.

Your own behavior style

The way you support your customer's need for Validation depends on your own behavior style.

- Salespeople who are Doers or Controllers favor results and authority. When providing Validation to customers, they'll talk about a company's position as a leader in the industry with quality products. However, if their customer is a Talker or a Supporter, it's important to include Validation based on brand reputation, company culture, and overall customer experience.

- Salespeople who are Talkers or Supporters need to give their Doer and Controller customers concrete examples of why the company and its products have earned such a trusted reputation.

Coaching Corner

Power thought

*The best way to get people to trust you
is to be a person people can trust.*
RON WILLINGHAM, FOUNDER, INTEGRITY SOLUTIONS

Questions and reflections

The Validate step is everything you say and do that causes people to trust you and believe your claims. Why do others trust you?

Think about who you are and what guides your moral compass. How can these be applied to each of the AID,Inc. steps?
   Include challenging situations, such as

- being truthful and authentic, even when it is difficult;

- allowing people to disagree without becoming defensive; and

- listening with respect and attention even if your values feel out of sync with the customer or the company.

Creating loyalty begins with creating value. How do you create more value for your customers?

Write down how you demonstrate value in three ways: with yourself, with your product/service, and with your organization. You might want to add these ideas to your pre-call notes.

10

Negotiating to Work Through Concerns and Objections

JUST AS LISA thought she was ready to close a sale, one of the decision-makers in the room announced, "It's too much money. We need more time to consider other options." Lisa was surprised and disappointed. Her instincts were to debate the point using price comparisons and performance reviews in order to change her customer's mind. Instead, she used her client's resistance to figure out what had been missed as she'd moved her customer through AID,Inc.

As she did so, it became obvious that during the Interview step, Lisa hadn't adequately uncovered budget parameters or fully demonstrated the value of the product. As a result, she had left the decision-makers with concerns about price and competition that they hadn't had a chance to articulate. Lisa asked if they could take a moment. This time, she faced the tough questions and feedback and listened without pushing back. In the end she was able to meet the customer's concerns and negotiate a sale.

. . . .

ONCE THE Demonstrate step is complete, it might feel like the customer is ready to make a decision. If things have gone well—let's assume they have—there will be nods or positive comments as you reach an agreement on why your product appears to be the best solution to meet their needs. However, you don't want to miss any clues concerning unsaid fears. This is why the Negotiate step is where you address concerns that stand in the way of a final decision. These could be objections or hesitations around risk that they need more time to discuss and solve. Or it could just be practical obstacles, like timing or availability, that need attention.

It can be challenging to hear pushback at this stage of the process. After all, you've come so far through the Interview and Demonstrate steps. The process can be especially trying during a complex sale, where major buying decisions are made by buying coalitions, not individuals. Instead of a couple of known decision-makers, you are now faced with a customer buying committee composed of a variety of decision-makers, influencers, and other interested parties, each with different priorities and needs.

You also need to be prepared when new stakeholders join the group mid-stream. An unanswered concern from one of them can derail the entire process. Shift your mindset to view concerns as welcomed feedback, not something to overcome.

Goals of the Negotiate Step

- Negotiate with confidence.
- Maintain composure when objections surface.
- Express empathy without agreeing.
- Anticipate and plan for objections or concerns.

Do I Really Have to Ask?

It's understandable to feel anxious about this step. Even the most experienced salespeople take a moment to remind themselves that there are compelling reasons to ask and address questions during the Negotiate step.

- Talking through concerns is a way to invite customers to get involved in solving their problems and work through their hesitancy to buy. When you get people to focus on possible solutions, they often sell themselves.

- Every objection and roadblock is an opportunity to deliver value. Now you can truly show your customers that you are there for their best interests, whether it results in a sale or not.

- You cannot respond to an objection that you know nothing about. And unresolved objections can seriously derail or stop a sale. This is unfortunate when the concerns can be addressed, perhaps through clarification or additional actions to reduce risk.

- When you show customers that you can see things from their point of view and imagine yourself in their place, you break down "we/they" barriers. Now you are both on the same side of the challenge and committed to working out a solution.

Slow Down to Win

Successful Negotiation isn't a strategy—it's a win-win attitude focused on helping customers make the best, most informed decisions.

The right time to Negotiate is when the customer indicates, "I want to use or recommend this product or service, but I have a concern."

The right way to respond is to say, "Okay then, we are going to slow this down so I can understand your concerns. I want you to be well equipped and informed to make this decision and able to justify it later."

You Go First!

What if no one states an objection? This certainly could be the case if your customer is a Doer and just wants to move forward. Negotiating, however, is a key step in the process, and it's there for a reason. This is another chance to show you are a trusted partner in their decision-making process. Even if nothing has been raised following the Demonstration, ask the customer or buying group to take a moment to review while you ask a few more questions:

- What other questions do you have?
- What other information do you need?
- What concerns, if any, do you have?
- What else do we need to discuss?

Acknowledge, Clarify, Respond

Let's say you're met with a concern. Take a deep breath and use the ACR system to guide your response:

The ACR System

ACKNOWLEDGE	**CLARIFY**	**RESPOND**
listen empathetically and non-defensively	understand the objection and identify additional concerns	with relevant data or additional information

Acknowledge the concern (don't debate or dismiss!): Listen empathetically and non-defensively. The natural tendency is to listen to respond. Instead, *really* listen to understand. Listening at this point can be one of the most significant actions in the sales interaction. Saying something like, "Thank you for sharing that concern" or even just "Okay" and totally focusing on the person goes a long way in building trust and respect.

Clarify by, for example, repeating what you've heard to make sure you understand the objection. It's even more important to explore the concern and ask questions to gain more insight. You might say, "Tell me more about that," "Can you clarify what you mean by that?" or "How significant is that?" People are more apt to listen and understand your point of view when you genuinely listen to and understand theirs.

Respond with relevant data and additional information. For example, this might be simply answering a question or correcting a misunderstanding. You may find the need to go back to the Demonstration and discuss the solution. Perhaps they don't fully believe your claims, and you can share a case study or resource to further Validate.

Adapting to Behavior Styles

Behavior Styles are often revealed when concerns or objections are expressed—those of your customers and your own. During the Negotiate step, learn to recognize the different emotions expressed when your customer faces a decision. Remember, to move forward, you need to find a way to bring all stakeholders together in a consensus of understanding around what needs to be addressed.

- Talkers don't enjoy making decisions, and emotion may cause them to fall into "decision paralysis." They'll welcome processes that help them move toward a decision that is workable for everyone.

- Doers like to make decisions, and they do so once they are convinced of the results. Give them what they need, and then get out of the way!

- Controllers want proof. Your assurance, even your good nature, isn't enough. Maybe there's an industry benchmarking report that backs up what you are telling them? Or a referral from a client in a similar industry?

- Supporters who are risk averse and resistant to change need to see a safe course ahead. What can you offer during the Negotiate step to help them move forward?

The High-EQ Salesperson

Your ability to negotiate without becoming defensive is influenced by emotional intelligence (EQ). EQ is the ability to recognize your emotions and their impact on your behavior. Using EQ to manage your emotions and relationships with others builds trust and rapport.

For example, someone with high EQ listens for and welcomes objections because while they are in the conversation, there is still an opportunity to explore solutions.

When trust and rapport are strong, Negotiation becomes a partnership to address customer concerns. But when trust and rapport are weak, almost any negotiation can become adversarial. Read more about EQ in Chapter 15.

Your own behavior style

Negotiation is an interaction with two sides, so naturally your own behavior style also affects it.

- As a Talker, the Negotiate step could be challenging because you'd prefer avoiding conflict. Now more than ever, you need to listen and ask for feedback. Silence while a customer considers a decision is okay.

- If you are a Doer, you are decisive when you know what you want. Negotiation is likely a step you'd rather skip! You'll have to exercise patience when dealing with those who need more time and detail before they move ahead.

- If your style is mostly Controller, you'll welcome the opportunity to provide additional data and proof. Be careful that you don't come across as annoyed that these concerns are being raised so late in the process.

- As a Supporter, you are great at drawing on the collective strengths of a group. Use this skill during the Negotiation. It will be invaluable when getting agreement on the next step and including everyone who needs to be involved in the final decision.

Coaching Corner

Power thought

The greatest form of persuasion is to understand how other people feel and then repeat back to them your understanding.
ATTRIBUTED TO CARL ROGERS, PSYCHOLOGIST

Questions and reflections

Can you clearly describe the advantages of your products versus competitive products? Role-play, working through common objections about competitive products.

What do you do ahead of a presentation to prepare for concerns?

Think about your behavior style and how you typically respond when an objection is given.

- Can you remember a specific example of how you adapted to your customer's style when responding to an objection?

- Can you remember a time when you didn't respond very well? What did you learn from that experience?

Closing to Ask for the Appropriate Action

LARS SENSED IT was time to ask for the Close. But when he posed the question, the buying manager said the dreaded words, "We'll need to show this to our chief procurement officer first. We'll get back to you." At that moment, Lars realized he'd lost control of the AID,Inc. process.

Next time Lars faced a similar situation, he changed his Closing question once he realized the Close would be a two-phase step. Instead of asking for the sale, he asked instead for the next group of decision-makers to be involved. It took an additional call, but Lars was part of the final meeting, and the Close went smoothly.

· · · · · · · · · · · · · · · ·

WHEN IS a customer ready to Close? The official answer: When you think you've successfully progressed to the point where a customer will say, "Yes, I want what you have and believe it will fill my needs." But as Lars discovered, you also have to be confident that you're asking the right question. Is it a final "Do we have an agreement?" or is there an action step that moves you closer to a sale but requires an additional call or two?

Ideally, everything you've asked and noted ahead of the Close helps you navigate the final step. For instance, don't just ask, "Who else is involved in the decision?" Do the research yourself. Source contacts, research connections, and look at past experience with customers of the same size or industry.

How do you tell whether they're ready for the Close step or still need a bit more encouragement? Detecting the signs is both an art and a science:

- **Art:** figuring out if you've earned the right to Close
- **Science:** knowing when and how to ask

The "art" means looking for buying signals. We'd love to give you the magic bullet for picking up the right buying signals, but it comes down to your ability to read each customer. Often, it is obvious that a customer is ready. They have expressed a need and agreed to the solution, and their questions have been answered. You observe how relaxed they look. Perhaps they lean forward, giving you a body language cue that they are engaged. Or if you're talking on the phone, their voice indicates excitement. You can almost hear them nodding their head.

The "science" part means knowing whether to ask for a decision (true Close) or an opinion (trial Close).

Goals of the Close Step

- Ask trial-closing questions.
- Listen to and reinforce each response.
- Be aware of buying signals.
- Ask for an appropriate Closing commitment.

Trial and Incremental Close

Trial-closing questions ask for an opinion rather than a decision. These questions can also be helpful when working with customers whose Behavior Styles are difficult to read. A trial Close helps you gauge the customer's level of interest. For example, "Have the data presented and our case studies convinced the group that our product can deliver the return on investment we talked about in our first meeting?"

There's also the incremental Close, in which you gain the first in a series of smaller commitments along the way. This was the case for Lars when he realized that his customer didn't have the authority to make a final decision. A next step could be something like the following:

- Gaining commitment for another meeting with the same person or another person or group who can make the actual decision
- Getting a recommendation to meet with someone else
- Gaining a commitment to try the product before making a more considerable commitment
- Getting approval from a committee that recommends your solution to a senior leader

Adapting to Behavior Styles

Behavior Styles become very clear during the Close—your customers' and your own.

Keep in mind the decision-making characteristics of your customer:

- Talkers want to ensure everyone around the table is happy with the decision. Look for ways to draw out this kind of group support.

- Doers may ask you to move forward without waiting for you to ask them. Be ready!

- Supporters and Controllers may move to the incremental Close. This could be one more step to get board approval or do a trial run. But note that each prefers an incremental Close for different reasons:

  - Supporters want to eliminate risks and pressure to buy. Be patient and talk through the risks and rewards.

  - Controllers may agree in principle but first want to weigh the risks against the costs. Find out what additional data or insight they need to do their analysis.

Your own behavior style

When you're Closing, make sure you know your own behavior style and watch how it affects you.

- If you know you have Doer characteristics, remember to take your time with this step, even though the decision to buy seems certain.

- If you are more of a Controller, don't stall the decision-making process with more details unless someone specifically requests them.

- Talkers and Supporters need to exercise patience when a decision is being made. Don't fill silence with more conversation. The good news if the sale doesn't Close: You'll find it easier to keep up the relationship until the next opportunity.

What Is the Next Actionable Step?

One of the greatest psychological needs of people is to be listened to without bias. Too often it seems someone is waiting for a chance to argue a point or jump in and resume talking.

When it looks like a Close isn't going to happen, think of it as your chance to show the customer you are a different kind of salesperson. You are focused on the relationship, not the transaction. Listen to their reasons for not moving ahead and think about other ways you can add value in the future. This is your chance to reinforce that you believe selling with integrity is identifying and satisfying customer needs and creating value for them, not trying to sell them something.

When the Customer Says No?
Develop a Nose for Opportunity

Healthy emotional intelligence tells you that you can't win them all. In some situations, you are going to need more time to get the business. Perhaps there are other relationships or contracts involved. Maybe they are doing business with their cousin Eddy and don't want to cause trouble in the family. Having a good nose for opportunity also means understanding when something has run its course.

This can be gut-wrenching, but it doesn't have to mean the end of the relationship you've built over weeks or months.

For starters, a no might mean "not now." Draw on your sales mindset and your emotional intelligence: Are you savvy and confident enough in the moment to turn this around? You could use the conversation to solidify yourself as the best second choice. Sometimes it's just a matter of time before your competitors falter.

Or maybe the no opens up a referral conversation like this: "It sounds like you believe in the value, but you can't move ahead right now. I appreciate your honesty. Before I go, would you be willing to connect me to someone else in your market space who might be another contact for me?"

What Is Your Mindset During the Close?

The Close step is a natural conclusion to the process when the first five steps have been completed well. There are no horns sounding or balloons falling from the sky and no happy dance (at least, that anyone can see). The step is directly related to your mindset: If this is the best solution for the customer, you and your customer decide on a positive action to take. This could be a sale or a call to action that advances the sale or creates mutual value for you and your customer.

This is a good time for an alignment check. How are you doing with each of the five dimensions in the Sales Congruence Model? Are one or more getting in your way of a successful Close?

- If you have solid values but a poor view of selling, you may not want to be seen as pushy and won't Close.

- If you have a positive view of selling but don't have a sound belief in the product, you might not ask for a commitment from your customer to use that product. You also might lack commitment to activities necessary to move them closer to a decision.

- Check in on your values and feelings of self-worth regarding your view of your abilities. Both influence your Closing. Do you have the confidence to ask trial-closing questions? Will your customer see you as a trusted advisor even if they decide to postpone the decision to buy from you right now? Do you know how to keep the relationship going after you hear "no"?

- When thinking about the Close step, refer to the Integrity Selling Values and Ethics in the Appendix. The values listed are at the core of values-based, customer-focused selling. You will have a successful Close, regardless of the final action, when you live by these values.

Selling is a permission-based interaction in which, as a service-minded, customer-focused person, you have a moral and ethical obligation to help your customers make the best choice. When you come to Close, the question on your mind should be, Did I help them make the right choice, even if it meant not making a sale?

Coaching Corner

Power thought

***Often when you think you're at the end of
something, you're at the beginning of something else.***
FRED ROGERS, CHILDREN'S TELEVISION HOST

Questions and reflections

What might cause a salesperson to hesitate to Close? Consider when you have the same hesitations and why.

When selling with integrity, you want to be convinced that the value to your customer exceeds their cost. How do you make sure this is the case?

What might be the incremental Closing steps for your product? Which ones lead to a buying decision? Which ones are still successful actions for moving forward?

Look at customer calls you've had where the initial answer was "no." How many of these resulted in an eventual sale? What did you do to make this happen? If they did not, is there something else you could have done differently?

Role-play Closing questions with a colleague, varying the behavior style of the decision-makers.

12

Preparing for
Sales Success

D O YOU REALLY have to spend a lot of time preparing for
sales calls?

Well, it depends. Do you want to sell something?

It's pretty much as simple as that.

There's a famous scene in Neil Simon's *The Odd Couple* where Oscar, who can't cook, suggests to Felix, who can cook, that he add gravy to save an overcooked meatloaf. When Felix asks where he will get gravy at eight o'clock at night, Oscar is bewildered. "I dunno, I thought it comes when you cook the meat."

Exasperated, Felix replies, "You don't know what you're talking about, Oscar... you've gotta *make* gravy; it doesn't *come!*"

It's the same in sales. Success doesn't just come. Your goal in every sales engagement is to maximize every interaction, whether it's a two-hour meeting or a short follow-up call. We've discussed how to do this through mindset and skillset. The third component of successful conversations is the disciplined process of preparation.

Like everything else, preparation has become more complicated. In the "olden days," salespeople prepared ahead of a call using index cards to keep notes about a customer's business and personal facts, like their birthday and the names of their children and their dog. When websites became an extension of a company's marketing and advertising efforts, salespeople gained another valuable resource: They could use "About Us" and "Meet Our Team" pages to brief them ahead of a call. Then came online platforms like LinkedIn and Facebook, where it was possible to look even deeper into a customer's network and find connections.

Today, we live and work in a world with easy access to more publicly available information than ever before. It's also a world where everyone has limited time and way too many distractions. Most buyers have already done their research before you contact them. They don't have patience for someone who's trying to catch up or is repeating something about their industry or market they already know. In addition, companies face a host of challenges and uncertainties that shift needs almost daily. Timing matters. They are looking for you to deliver value and want you to do so quickly.

The bottom line: If you can demonstrate from your first engagement that you have put in the effort to gain an understanding of the customers you are meeting and what's happening in *their* world—not last year, but this month—you have a tremendous competitive advantage.

What Does Preparation Include?

Now that you've completed all six steps of AID,Inc., what are you going to do to prepare for your next sales engagement? This chapter highlights some of the tools and benefits of good preparation.

As we discussed earlier, AID,Inc. provides a disciplined process for moving through your first and subsequent sales conversations. Preparation is required for each step in a call to maximize the time you spend with all decision-makers in a group. When you are prepared, you can respond to your customers' questions and feel like you are having a dialogue. When you're not prepared, you tend to fill that space with a lot of talking.

Everyone believes that they prepare, but effective preparation takes time and commitment. Think of it like detective work. You are looking beyond assumptions and general information that anyone can find. You need clues about what's happening in an industry, in a business, or even inside a customer's head.

The information may be industry-related, market-related, technical, or anecdotal, such as a case study. But you need enough at your fingertips that's relevant—each time—for the purpose of the call. As you compile the information, realize that some of it may not make sense until you ask more questions or do more digging.

For example:

- During the Approach, preparation can help you uncover shared interests and networks with your customer and discover relevant personal or professional connections. All of this can help you establish rapport.

- During the Interview, preparation means preparing mentally and creating high-impact questions that keep the conversation moving forward. Now you are listening and asking questions that create thoughtful responses.

- During the Demonstration, preparation involves research to know how to position the benefits of your proposed solutions so your client buys in to the value you can deliver. This may also include resources you have ready to Validate your product and your company.

- During the Negotiate step, preparation is needed to respond to feedback from the previous call. The data you've gathered satisfies the Controllers in the group, and the testimonials you've found put the Supporters at ease. You also prepare by anticipating concerns before they're raised and drafting possible responses. Preparation at this step prevents you from becoming reactive, which is emotional, rather than responsive, which is logical.

- During the Close, you've prepared ahead by drafting trial-closing questions for each commitment you'd like to achieve at this step. Or maybe, using clues you've picked up along the way, you're prepared for an incremental Close. As you move toward the Close, conversations will proceed naturally to actions that everyone agrees are the best steps forward.

Pre-Call Notes

Keeping information in your head rarely works. You won't remember as much as you'd like, so you won't be fully prepared for the unexpected. Pre-call notes record where you are in the AID,Inc. process, what you know so far, what you need to find out, and what your objectives are.

This means you also need a process for recording what happens during each sales engagement so you can review, update, share, and use it throughout the steps in the sales process.

Each pre-call planning document should record the following details:

- Customer's name (if known)

- Behavior style notes (see the Behavior Styles Checklist in the Appendix)

- A clearly defined call objective (specific to each call)

- A Statement of Intent for your customer (more on this later)

- Notes, questions, and resources, depending on where you are in the AID,Inc. process. For example:

  - Several well-thought-out questions (Interview)

  - Features translated into benefits (Demonstrate)

  - Testimonials, company credentials, and case studies (when there is a need to Validate)

  - Anticipated objections with answers backed up with data, resources, etc. (Negotiate)

  - Trial-closing questions and a specific Closing commitment (Close)

Various pre-call sales tools help collect and collate information in an organized manner. Many salespeople use a digital format, which can be easily shared with their manager. Others use paper-based tools, either because they don't have an online CRM or the institution needs to meet specific privacy regulations.

Use whatever works for you. The goal is to build the preparation habit into your overall selling approach. And if you don't get too far through the process in one engagement, there might not be too much to add. That's okay. Checking your notes is part of the overall discipline.

To Keep It, Write It Down

Consider the following: Regardless of age, our short-term memories can hold up to seven pieces of information simultaneously, and even then, only for around twenty seconds. Each of us also carries an average of 70,000 thoughts in a day.

Just finished a meeting? Fifty percent of the information presented will be forgotten within an hour and, on average, 70 percent in twenty-four hours.

The solution to this problem is simple: To keep it, write it down. Neuroscience tells us that not only does writing things down help us remember them, but it also improves recall of essential information. In short, taking notes makes your mind more efficient by allowing you to focus on what's most important.

One study found that when people weren't taking notes in class, they remembered just as many unimportant facts as they did essential facts. But when people were taking notes, they retained many more important facts and many fewer unimportant facts.

Setting a Purpose or Call Objective

Every engagement, call, email, or video chat needs a purpose to guide the conversation and set the tone. Use your pre-call notes to determine your ideal outcome. What do you want out of your call? Be precise. For example:

- Draw out feedback and concerns about something you've delivered or presented.

- Find out if additional decision-makers will be part of the process.

- Have the group agree on three or four priority needs.

- Follow up on a previous meeting with specific information, examples, or resources you promised to bring.

- Get agreement for a second/next call.

- Get a commitment to try the product before making a final decision.

The purpose will change depending on where you are in AID,Inc. For example:

- Before the Approach step, you're trying to get an appointment with a new customer. Your first call's goal is "to build rapport to gain a second call."

- At the Interview and Demonstrate steps, you set goals like "find out their greatest challenge," "prioritize their need," and "get feedback on the product."

- At the Negotiate step, you'd love to move closer to the sale, but in your pre-call notes, perhaps you wrote down a risk raised by one of the decision-makers. This time, your goal is to present new information that Validates the product and satisfies the concern.

- When you reach the Close, your goal is to ask for an appropriate Closing commitment. As the meeting progresses, perhaps you can tell that they are ready to buy the first three products you've recommended. You ask for the sale, and the answer is "yes."

Statement of Intent

Once you've set a purpose for the call, turn it into a Statement of Intent for your customer. This statement clearly communicates why you are meeting with them. It doesn't matter how simple it sounds; everyone will appreciate the efficiency and clarity (especially the Doers and Controllers around the table!). Here are a few examples:

- My call today is to answer your questions about the product we demonstrated last week.

- The purpose of today's meeting is for me to understand your business better and identify who else I should meet with to learn more.

- What I'd like to understand today is how supply chain issues affect your business.

- We have two new individuals joining the meeting today. I want to brief them on what we've discussed and then ask for their input so we can be aligned on the most significant needs.

- As you requested, I've brought in a technical expert from our team to listen to the valid concerns you expressed about product repairs and maintenance last time.

- Today, we'll walk through how we can help you make training simpler and more accessible.

- We want to learn more about your organization's purpose. Tell us about what's most important to your brand. How is what you do reflected in your vision statement?

Post-Call Analysis

Assessing how the call went is another form of preparation. A post-call analysis prepares you for the next call. Your post-call report should include the following:

- An honest self-analysis of progress made during the call. A simple format is, What went well, and why? and, What didn't go well, and why?

- Notes for follow-up: what needs to be done, when, and by whom

- The objective of the next call

Unfortunately, too many post-call analyses are missed or delayed. We get that. If the call didn't go so well, you will likely want to put the experience behind you. If the engagement was great, you're feeling invincible. You're also probably pressed for time. You figure you'll remember what took place or what you promised for the next meeting. This almost never happens.

Write down what happened as soon as you can. If it's easier, dictate notes to your phone and use a text-to-speech tool so you can put them into your report. The goal is to create an accurate record of what happened. If things go well, you'll know why for next time. If the conversation was difficult, you'll have a more balanced memory of what happened.

How Much Is Enough?

For a cold call, pre-call planning may be limited to general information about the industry and market and some typical questions. Details on each customer won't be researched unless the cold call leads to further engagement. But even a few moments of preparation can change an awkward introduction into one that's focused and energetic.

For an incoming inquiry, preparation may be difficult because you don't know the person or situation. For that reason, it's important to ask questions and pick up on cues such as tone of voice, pace, words, and energy level. This can indicate their behavior style and provide direction for the sales conversation.

In a cross-selling or upselling scenario, your preparation can leverage prior conversations and reference previous pre- and post-call plans and analyses.

Throughout a complex sale, preparation is an ongoing process as various stakeholders and stakeholder groups are brought into the conversation and, over weeks and months, circumstances change. In these instances, you need a new pre-call plan each time to ensure new participants go through the full AID,Inc. process.

In addition to pre-call planning, preparation for a complex sale by the sales leader and team typically includes a strategic overview and plan, with notes on the following:

- The long-term goals you hope to accomplish
- What you know about the buying process and decision criteria
- How to build relationships with all stakeholders who influence a buying decision

Preparation and Getting in Sync

We mentioned previously the importance of confidence, and how it increases when there is congruence between your internal beliefs: your view of selling, view of your abilities, values, commitment to activities, and belief in product.

Preparation is one of the best ways to pull these into alignment. When you know the industry, the market, and the products well, you improve your view of your abilities and your belief in the products. When you take time to know your customers, including their Behavior Styles and roles in an organization, your view of selling shifts to how to best meet their needs and not just sell. As a result, you commit to doing the activities necessary to prepare.

Preparation Means Confidence

One of the biggest mistakes we see salespeople make is thinking they don't have enough time to prepare ahead of a call (whether it's by phone, face-to-face meeting, video, email, or text). But preparation is one of the best ways to demonstrate to your customer what you think of them.

Here's how one of our trainers puts it: "How important is that person sitting in front of you? If they truly are important to you—and you care about them—then preparation has to be more than grabbing some information that everyone already knows. The customer can tell if this is what you've done. Conversations take various twists and turns, and often you don't get the answer you're expecting. When they ask a question or make a comment and you've prepared well, you can respond without it being awkward—if you haven't, you'll risk making them feel unimportant!"

Coaching Corner

Power thought

I believe luck is preparation meeting opportunity. If you hadn't been prepared when the opportunity came along, you wouldn't have been lucky.
OPRAH WINFREY, TALK SHOW HOST

Questions and reflections

Do you have time for proper preparation? If not, what needs to happen to change this?

What is your process following a sales engagement? Describe when and how you record what happened during the meeting, including notes for follow-up before the next call.

What you say near the beginning of the sales conversation helps the customer decide if they see value in spending time with you. Take time to write out a few Statements of Intent you might use in the future.

What do you do mentally to prepare for a meeting? What if the meeting is just a five-minute conversation?

Ten Techniques for Outstanding Preparation

ONE OF OUR sales trainers was sitting on an airplane next to a heart surgeon. "Tell me," he said to the physician, "when a sales rep comes to visit you, what makes it a good experience?" The physician paused for a moment and replied, "They bring value." Our trainer nodded and asked, "What do you mean by that?" "Well," he said, "when they see me, they are prepared. They are thinking about questions concerning my patient demographics, and they discuss procedures that are related to helping me improve my practice. I can read brochures and papers about the equipment and devices they represent. However, they bring real value to me when they come prepared to help me help my patients."

So then our sales trainer asked, "And what about the others—the reps who aren't prepared in that way?"

The physician didn't hesitate to respond. "They are a waste of time. They show up at the most inopportune times and then ask the same questions every single time. So I don't see them."

· · · · · · · · · · · · · · · ·

NO ONE wants to be a waste of time! Preparation needs to go beyond what is expected to elevate your conversations to "stand-out." The online world is a gold mine of opportunity for the salesperson ready to spend some time digging it out. This, of course, is in addition to the wealth of industry and marketing reports, analyses, and insights available for anyone with moderately good research skills.

The following ten suggestions will help take you there. A goal is assigned to each, which you can tie back to a step in AID,Inc.

1. Look for the Six Degrees of Separation

Goal: Identify points of personal connection to begin the relationship (Approach).

There's a chance you share a connection with someone: an organization, a cause, an interest. Find out where your networks overlap to build initial rapport during the Approach step. Shared connections provide a degree of legitimacy and a way to start a conversation beyond "I'm here to sell you something!"

- Google their name and see what you find. You may be interested in the same charity, you are both hockey moms, or your children attend the same college.

- Are they active in online writing or responding to social media posts? Find out what they say and read in topic-specific forums and industry groups.

- Check membership lists from your alma mater, industry and professional associations, and current customers. You could find someone to ask about their interests and position in the company.

- Check for videos of them presenting or being interviewed to see what you can learn. This also can be an excellent way to uncover clues about their behavior style.

Prep tip: If you don't have an opportunity to prepare, listen for opportunities to uncover new information. What do you hear that can be turned into a high-impact question instead of the same thing everyone else is asking?

2. Make Yourself Relevant

Goal: Be ready to ask about and respond to what you hear (Interview).

To make it immediately clear that your intent is to create value, not just sell, you have to do more than comment in a general way about the state of the economy or rehash what you've read on a home page. Use your preparation to show that you understand the complexities of their business, their industry, and the market they sell in.

- Through press releases, you can find out news about products, innovations, awards, new employees, or departments. Congratulate the customer on the specific news and ask for updates and details.

- Governmental regulatory agencies will often post policy changes on their websites and social media. Check these for the latest industry updates so you can stay informed and relevant to your customer.

- Blogs give insight into the company's thought leadership. What are they writing about? Your customer may also be highlighted or interviewed in third-party blogs, podcasts, or news features.

- Career sections tell you who they are hiring. Job postings give direct clues about strategic planning, new products and services, and current priorities.

- Current and past annual reports reveal recent organizational changes, financial health, and strategic planning.

- Posts on social media platforms often provide more details. For example, in general, bios on a website aren't as detailed as resumes and posts on LinkedIn.

Prep tip: Identifying trends is important, but which ones are high priorities to your customer? If they are in the fleet industry, are they looking to reduce maintenance costs or struggling because they don't have enough skilled drivers? Go beyond the website home page or what you assume is going on. Go deep into the inside pages for clues about what's happening in their organization and why.

3. Sell Past the Sale

Goal: Find out who the end users of your customer's products are and what their challenges and needs are (Interview and Demonstrate).

If your customers have customers, you have additional pre-work to do. You need to look beyond the needs and challenges of just your direct customer and consider what impact your solutions might have on the value they provide to their customers.

Prep tip: You are most valuable to your customer if you enhance the way they provide value to their customers in some way.

4. Step Into the Industry

Goal: Be an invaluable source of information regarding their industry or market (Demonstrate and Validate).

Innovation, digitization, automation, customization, commoditization, regulation, and on it goes—we live in rapidly changing times for businesses, and that means no single executive can be an expert in everything. These complexities today's decision-makers are facing represent your greatest opportunity.

According to one survey, 64 percent of B2B buyers want vendors who demonstrate knowledge of their company and offer insights into their problems, and 62 percent want salespeople to demonstrate experience with and understanding of their industry.

If you are a sales manager, your preparation includes strategizing with your team ahead of a sales meeting. What are the top industry challenges? Talk about how these might affect their customers. The more you know about the industry you sell in, the more valuable you become.

- Search for current trend reports from sources recognized in the industry (for example, Gartner, IBISWorld, white papers from major consulting firms). Pay attention to mergers and acquisitions, new product entrants, technological advancements, and changing legislation.

- Identify priorities so you know where to start a conversation. For example, regulatory concerns rank high for utilities, so what can you learn about recent state changes?

- Spend time on trade association websites. In addition to helping you identify and make connections with industry leaders, these are extremely valuable resources for trends and emerging issues.

- Subscribe to thought leaders' newsfeeds, webinars, and posts for an insider view of the conversation going on in the industry.

- See if a seminar or online event is coming up that you can attend. Many companies hold virtual roundtable discussions for their executives, customers, employees, like-minded peers, and investors.

- Interview different stakeholders during the sales process.

- When researching, look for stories from those who benefit from the organization's work. You can use those examples in a conversation or introductory email.

Prep tip: When selling to installers and contractors, be aware that one of their biggest challenges is keeping up with changing regulations and efficiency standards. Sure, you can offer the best equipment—just like everyone else—but if you become a knowledge source on industry issues, you'll be able to ask intelligent questions about changes affecting their customers or trends they need to know about to stay ahead of the competition.

5. Prep Your Team

Goal: Bring your knowledge experts into the AID,Inc. process (Demonstrate and Negotiate).

Here's an example of a kind of situation that happens all too often: A salesperson working with a customer that provides industrial solvents to the automotive industry has just scheduled a meeting with the heads of three departments. Since the salesperson isn't a chemist, they bring in a technical expert from the sales team to address concerns. Before anyone speaks, this person starts a lengthy presentation, rarely looking up at the group and only pausing when she wants to share more data.

Preparation is crucial when you have invited a knowledge expert to a meeting. Your expert is part of the sales team. They have been waiting for their moment to talk about what they like to talk about—the great product. However, it's up to you to synchronize them with the sales process, not just the subject matter.

Prep tip: Technical and brand experts need to be briefed in a pre-call meeting on what was covered in previous calls. Share with them priorities that need to be addressed and the strategy for engagement (in other words, the kinds of information and data the group would welcome, as well as Behavior Styles of the people involved).

6. Know the Competition

Goal: Be able to present the difference and the value (Demonstrate and Validate).

Do what it takes to know your competitors' strengths and weaknesses. Be honest with yourself if there isn't a significant difference. Knowing there is product parity motivates you to look for other ways to talk about value. When customers ask you, "Is there a difference?" you can answer them positively, without hesitation, because you know where the value is for them.

This can also be a great coaching opportunity for sales managers. How can you improve the team's ability to identify unarticulated customer needs? What does it mean to deliver value beyond the products and services offered? For example, in highly competitive industries such as fintech and pharma-ceuticals, being responsive and engaged may be all you can offer at first.

Prep tip: Know more about your competition than what's on their website. One of our clients keeps every product sold by their competitors in a room at the head office. With a hands-on understanding of what's being presented to their customers, salespeople can see and experience ways to dif-ferentiate their products.

7. Be Ready for Indifference

Goal: Uncover the competition you didn't know was there (Interview).

Sometimes the competition is your customer's attitude of indifference. Your customer has always done something in a specific way or used a certain product from the same vendor. Or perhaps you are selling something new, like a piece of technology, and your customer doesn't realize the difference it could make in their manufacturing process.

Indifference, however, can often uncover new oppor-tunities. What did you hear during the Interview step that provided insight into an operational aspect of the business? Find ways to talk about the risks of not making a change.

You also may find clues by looking at who they are hiring or online reviews that reveal challenges their customers face. Once these issues are discussed, you can move to the out-comes they might enjoy if a change is made.

Prep tip: The GAP Model in Chapter 7 is an excellent way to prepare for indifference. Use the questions in the bottom half of the graphic that ask about risks and concerns and about benefits and rewards (see also the GAP Analysis Questions in the Appendix). These are designed to help the customer answer the question, "Why should I care?"

8. Wow Your Customer by Being a Different Kind of Salesperson

Goal: Be ready with the right resources at the right place and the right time (Validate).

Issues of trust are at an all-time high. Prepare to demonstrate one or more of the trust attributes discussed in Chapter 9: connection, authenticity, respect, and integrity.

For example, if you can cite a recent trend report, data, or case study that frames your understanding of your customer's business, you start to build trust as someone who delivers value (connection, authenticity). If you believe the product they want to buy from you isn't the best choice for their needs at the time and you tell them that, they will trust your judgment from then on (respect, integrity).

Prep tip: You need a healthy level of sales confidence to be bold enough to say things a customer may not want to hear. Preparation gives you this confidence.

9. When the Chips Are Down, Be Creative

Goal: Find ways to connect when the rug is pulled out from under you (Approach).

The COVID years were a great example of how preparation meant a brand-new way of looking at a challenge. Almost overnight, salespeople found out they no longer could meet with customers face-to-face. For many, their sales congruence was knocked out of balance. Few were used to the technology to sell online, let alone the technical and communication skills that went along with virtual meetings.

As sales teams rushed to fill the gap, clever salespeople began to reshape their beliefs by focusing on questions like, "How can I make selling virtually as engaging as face-to-face?" "Are there benefits to meeting differently?" "Where can I learn this new technology and increase my value to my customers by helping them adapt?"

People got creative. Within months, we saw virtual lunches, online conferences, celebratory events, and even meetings where food and drinks were sent ahead to the participants. In one instance, a sales team delivered children's videos with milk and cookies to the door where their client— a parent—was stuck working at home. The salesperson's objective was simple: Find a creative way to have an uninterrupted conversation.

Prep tip: You can't prepare for every circumstance. When faced with the unknown, listen to your clients' fears, listen to the conversation in your head, and listen to your team. Then ask the question, How can I add value in this new environment?

10. Be Mentally Prepared

Goal: Enter the call with confidence and congruence (all steps).

Researchers agree that mental preparation, when combined with physical preparation, positively affects performance. For example, let's say you have a conflict with your boss ahead of a meeting where you planned to Demonstrate the product benefits to a group of decision-makers. How does this affect your day? Or perhaps you just lost a sale the day before, or one of your best customers called to express disappointment with a piece of equipment you sold them last month. How does this affect your week?

Prep tip: Regardless of how your day has gone so far, take a few minutes to do the following ahead of each meeting:

- Visualize a successful customer interaction—beliefs influence outcomes!
- Think about how customers are going to benefit from using your product.

Preparation and Mindset

What we think about "under the surface"—our achievement drive, sense of purpose, and the level of success we feel is deserved—accounts for more than 90 percent of our feelings, beliefs, and behaviors. This is powerful insight.

Fortunately, our brains are adaptable, so we can use techniques such as self-talk to help remove negative beliefs and replace them with positive ones. It doesn't happen overnight, but continuous practice can make a big difference in your mindset.

Take time to think about your alignment in the five dimensions of congruence. Do you have confidence in your abilities? Do you have confidence in your understanding of your customers? Will the product deliver value and change circumstances for your customer in a positive way? What is your view of selling and values? Do you believe you are there *for and with* them, not to sell *to* them?

Technology and the Modern Sales Engagement

When video calls became the only way salespeople could meet and present to customers, it was an abrupt shift and, for some, a steep learning curve. Now that virtual has become simply another channel for interacting with customers, it's up to salespeople to make sure they're optimizing how and when they use the different methods available to them.

Today's sales teams are expected to combine virtual meetings with face-to-face interactions to create better engagement experiences with their customers. Use technology when it's the better choice—the more effective or practical choice—in your particular circumstance.

Virtual Skillset

Virtual meetings require some specific preparation tips. From the moment your customer receives a link ahead of a meeting, you want them to feel at ease and know that you will manage the call without technological glitches or excuses.

- Check audio levels and internet strength.
- Learn different platforms so you can adapt to what your customer uses.
- Use proper lighting and sound equipment and a professional (or blurred) background.
- Have materials ready to share and a clean desktop.
- Check your appearance through the camera ahead of time. Specific patterns on clothes and jewelry can be distracting on camera. Be honest about what you see!

See the Appendix for a list of Virtual Meeting Tips.

Connecting with the Reluctant Buyer

Many customers today are what we describe as "reluctant buyers." Salespeople experience the impact of such reluctance every day. They see how buyers hesitate to move forward on a decision for reasons ranging from budget freezes to uncertainty about the future to fear of the unknown. Given the major shifts that have been happening in the world and in sales over the past decade, this reluctance isn't surprising. Their fear and the risks they face are real.

Customer reluctancy, however, doesn't mean customers don't need salespeople. They need you more than ever to help them think through a solution from all angles. They are looking for conversations that help them come up with ideas they may not have considered on their own, or to change their perspective so they can move past where they are now to where they want to be.

Effective preparation equips you with what you need to bring to the sales call. More data, research, case studies, or testimonials on their own don't translate into helping salespeople have better conversations with customers. If you want to move the reluctant buyer, you need to connect with clients on an emotional level. Conversations need to move beyond questions about their current state and show the benefit of change and risk of the status quo.

For example, you could ask, "What's your greatest challenge?" but a more emotionally intelligent question would be, "What might be the ripple effect if you could increase productivity by 20 percent?" Now you are directly addressing their risk and benefits.

Empathetic, values-based conversations like these take practice. How do you know if you are doing this well? How do you evaluate whether your conversations are distracting or holding your customer back? What kind of response are you listening for, and how do you adjust your conversation?

Managers need to be able to coach salespeople to have better conversations with their customers. And the secret of how to have an effective coaching conversation isn't reserved for just managers. As a salesperson, the more you learn about coaching conversations, the better you can evaluate your own performance. When you've experienced a successful call, you can have a conversation with yourself about what moved your reluctant buyer to a place of confidence. What kind of preparation helped you think from your buyer's perspective?

All of this brings us to the last kind of conversation—coaching conversations.

Coaching Corner

Power thought

It doesn't matter what you're trying to accomplish. It's all a matter of discipline.
WILMA RUDOLPH, OLYMPIC SPRINTER

Questions and reflections

Where do you find the most helpful information when preparing to talk with your customers?

During preparation, how do you identify new or cross-selling opportunities?

Think about a virtual meeting that went well. Why was this the case? Can you duplicate what happened at your next meeting?

How can you keep up the energy level during a virtual meeting?

PART THREE

COACHING CONVERSATIONS

FOR SKILL AND WILL

With each success, our belief boundaries expand, and we can reach a higher level of achievement.

14

Sales Coaching

RAJ WAS A VERY successful salesperson. He was so successful that his company promoted him to sales manager. Now Raj has a salesperson who reports to him, and she is under pressure to meet an annual sales quota.

Every two weeks, Raj checks in with the salesperson. He asks about her progress and if she is having difficulty with the steps in AID,Inc. Raj shares what has always worked for him. He shares call reports so she can see what she needs to do to get the job done.

The salesperson, however, is struggling. There's no engagement in her interviews. She jumps to the Demonstrate step in AID,Inc. before properly defining her customers' needs, and at Close, she avoids directly asking for the business. "What else can I do?" asks Raj, frustrated by his lack of progress with her. "I've gone on sales calls with her to point out what she's doing wrong, but nothing seems to work."

Both Raj and his salesperson are stuck.

The salesperson is working hard to do her best. But her confidence is slipping, and she's questioning whether she should even be in sales. Raj is discouraged because he doesn't understand why she isn't listening.

. . . .

DOES THIS sound familiar to you? Maybe you work for a manager like Raj who keeps pushing you to do better even though you have your own reasons for why the products aren't selling. Or, as a manager, you are saying the same thing repeatedly to your salespeople and expecting different results.

Managers and their sales reps find themselves in this kind of situation every day. Typically, sales managers use time with their people to review sales and pipeline activity and recommend ways to increase sales. As a performance management measure, the conversation is tied to a number, not the person. It doesn't uncover what's really going on.

The good news here is that all of this is fixable.

There are reasons why a salesperson isn't asking for a decision. Understanding what's happening and how to get a different result starts with a manager sitting down with a salesperson and asking questions related to the emotional aspects of selling: "What's happening here?" "Why are you only asking this question?" "How do you feel about the value of our solutions?"

We refer to it as a coaching approach rather than performance management.

Throughout the book, we've used the Coaching Corner at the end of each chapter to highlight the kinds of questions you can ask to develop your insights or the insights of your salespeople. We've looked at conversations with yourself that help shift mindset and conversations with customers that focus on listening and building loyal relationships. Some of the questions may have been easy to answer, but others need deeper discussion.

This is where coaching plays a fundamental role. Coaching is the human side of selling, and when applied to sales conversations, it helps salespeople ask the right questions, listen more effectively, enhance self-awareness, clarify goals, express belief, and build confidence. You may be able to incorporate such conversations into all your sales activities on your own, but you don't have to do this alone. This is where managers trained in coaching play a pivotal role in an organization's success.

Once you recognize how to shift to a coaching approach, you will know what to do—whether you are a salesperson or a manager. And by adopting a few concepts from the coaching model, you can start to turn things around.

What Is Coaching?

A global study led by Integrity Solutions showed that only a quarter of those surveyed had a standard definition of coaching. So, let's start with defining what we mean by coaching, specifically sales coaching.

When you think of coaching, think conversation. At its core, coaching uses conversation to develop a person's awareness and clarity around what they are doing and why. It's not necessarily about correcting or fixing. It's about listening and helping people transform any mindsets and beliefs that could be holding back their success. This can only be done through a process that applies techniques common to all coaching:

- Questions that draw out what needs to change or be adjusted
- Active listening to understand rather than assume or advise

As one of our lead coaches likes to remind his team, coaching helps managers see through a different lens and ask the salesperson, "What do *you* think you should do, and how do *you* think you should solve the problem?" Then, together, they set the goal, plan how to get there, and put in place the best process to stay accountable.

You Can Improve Your Coaching Skills

Coaching as a practice is broad, with specific categories for types of coaching. Developmental coaching, for instance, uses formal assessments, past experiences, and feedback to reveal the root of the mindset problem or insecurity. Through a developmental coaching approach, the coach helps people equip themselves with new skills and thought structures to tackle issues independently.

Integrity Solutions offers comprehensive coaching training. Scan this QR code for more information about the Integrity Coaching® program.

And Now, Sales Coaching

For this chapter, we are going to talk specifically about sales coaching, which focuses on behaviors that apply to the customer experience. The questions apply whether you are a sales professional or a sales manager coaching a team. These behaviors include both mindset and skillset conversations that ask the following:

- Are you doing the necessary activities to discover what your customer really needs and help them make a decision using AID,Inc.?

- If you're not doing the activities necessary to get results, what's getting in the way in terms of mindset?

The answers could be straightforward, based purely on the need for more training or knowledge. Often, however, they overlap and influence each other.

If you are skipping the Validate step and going right to Close, what's going on here? Maybe you haven't been trained in the importance of repeating AID,Inc. steps when new stakeholders join the conversation. Not following the steps, however, could also be a symptom related to mindset. For some reason, you're resisting what needs to be done before moving to the next step. It's why we often describe mindset as a "will" issue. Is there a confidence issue with the product that's blocking your willingness to ask for the sale? Is it a values issue that's making you so uncomfortable that you avoid making a call?

Coaching That Addresses Both Skill and Will

Selling issues can be divided into "skill" and "will" issues. Many selling issues are a combination of both.

"Skill" issues apply to using AID,Inc., preparation activities, and how to relate to different Behavior Styles.

Coaching to sales skills includes training in conversations; asking direct/indirect questions; and learning Behavior Styles, product knowledge, account strategy, the sales process, and methodologies (AID,Inc.).

"Will" issues are matters of mindset that emerge when the five elements of the Sales Congruence Model aren't in sync. These have to do with barriers such as how you view what you do as a salesperson, what you feel confident about, what you believe about yourself, and how external issues around you are influencing your behavior.

Coaching to sales mindset includes self-assessment and coaching to the Sales Congruence Model: understanding self-imposed barriers and influences, building belief in product and abilities, increasing achievement drive, committing to activities, and aligning your values with your view of selling.

Who Has Time to Coach These Days?

We often hear managers say, "I don't have time to coach. Letting people learn from experience and find their own path is a luxury I can't afford. It's easier to tell someone how to do it so they can get on with selling."

Take heart. In the long run, the coaching time you invest will be well worth it. Not only are there benefits to having your employee do the thinking required to solve the problem, but there are also several strategies you can use to make coaching part of your routine.

Use the following to fit coaching into your management activities:

Scheduled coaching sessions: Make a coaching session part of your regularly planned meetings. These can be done in person, on the telephone, or via video.

Coaching Moments™: These are informal check-ins following a call or during a ride-along where you give feedback "on the spot." Frequently providing feedback in this way lets the person know how they are doing in the moment. Maybe they did something very well, or perhaps you want to know why they skipped a step in the process.

Take time in the moment so the occasion isn't forgotten when everyone gets back to work. If the issue is a sign of a bigger problem, the sooner it can be addressed, the better.

Spot the Symptom and Test Yourself

Following are some sales challenges we see repeatedly. They also represent various coaching opportunities. You may identify with them as the salesperson, the manager, or some of both! These summaries highlight the symptom and then provide coaching questions to get to the real heart of the problem.

As you read them, ask yourself if you have ever done this. Do you have people on your team who do this? You may also use the sample questions to "sales coach" yourself or your team.

Getting stuck on the price question

A salesperson selling in a very competitive market is continually being asked about price before they get through the Interview step. If the price doesn't compare well with a competitor's, the sale shuts down. Once this happens, it's too late to go back and ask those customer-focused needs questions.

What happened here? "How much will it cost?" are dreaded words when they are asked before you can show value beyond price. Customers often jump to price if they don't believe a salesperson is listening to them or they don't immediately see value in who you are and what you are selling. They put your company in the same category as "all the others who are just trying to sell, sell, sell."

Price is important, but you need to help them understand why focusing on price alone may not be in their best interest.

Is this a skillset or mindset issue, or a bit of both? The only way to tell is to ask coaching questions, such as these:

- What do you listen for so you can detect early in the process what might represent significant value for this customer?

- What is your view of selling? Can you articulate the value you bring, besides the product?

- How do you demonstrate to the customer that you are listening?

- What do you do to pre-empt a discussion on price?

- How do you handle a question about price?

Asking predictable or low-impact questions

A salesperson has carefully researched the company and prepared questions to ask about the business, but the Approach and Interview fail to move to the next step. The customer tends to give one-word answers like "sometimes" and "maybe," and few provide insight into their needs. Soon, the customer starts to put up barriers, and the salesperson loses confidence.

What happened here? When customers give short answers and don't engage, it's often a symptom of the salesperson asking close-ended and low-impact questions. In addition, there may be a behavior-style mismatch. The customer may be a Doer who expects you've already researched the "what" and "how" questions.

Is this a skillset or mindset issue, or a bit of both? The only way to tell is to ask coaching questions, such as these:

- Help me understand how you prepare for your sales calls.

- What clues do you look for in terms of behavior style, and then how do you adapt?

- How do you use the GAP Model?

- Can we role-play some GAP Model questions?

Getting stumped on a behavior style

A salesperson selling medical devices is standing at his customer's door, waiting for the customer to return to his office. The surgeon walks purposefully down the hall and, with barely a nod, sits down at his desk with his back to the salesperson and starts checking his computer. The salesperson tries to engage with him, but there's little traction. He reports back to his manager, who asks him what the surgeon's behavior style is. The salesperson realizes he failed to consider that the surgeon has a Controller style. Next time he visits, he changes his approach. He starts talking about recent case studies and the kinds of results doctors can expect. The surgeon turns in his chair and says, "So, how's your week been?"

What happened here? We all bring different Behavior Styles to the decision-making process. The salesperson is a Talker, but the decision-maker is a Controller. Controllers take their time carefully reviewing a situation, gathering facts, and planning what they are going to ask. If Talkers don't adapt to a Controller style, for example, they may not move past the Approach step.

Is this a skillset or mindset issue, or a bit of both? The only way to tell is to ask coaching questions, such as these:

- What clues help you recognize a customer's style?

- Tell me about the communication tendencies of your own behavior style.

- Which behavior style do you find most challenging to work through concerns with, and why?

- How are you adapting to the customer's behavior style when you demonstrate the product benefits?

- What immediate clues help reveal a customer's style?

- What kind of information or data do you prepare for a Supporter versus a Talker?

Not asking for the sale

A sales manager attends a meeting with his salesperson where everyone expected the client to sign. It is clear the customer recognizes the value of the product. Stakeholders even nod their heads as the discussion wraps up. But near the end of the call, the salesperson smiles and says, "Let us know if you are interested."

The manager is alarmed. He's seen this behavior from the salesperson before. They're reluctant to ask for an action step that would move them closer to a sale. The manager tells them what he's observed and instructs them, "Next time, I want you to ask for the business." The salesperson is annoyed and rationalizes that it was up to the customer to decide, not them.

What happened here? The sales manager can instruct his salesperson to ask for the business, but wielding authority isn't going to get to the root of the problem. Maybe his salesperson doesn't want to come across as pushy or needs to know the right words to use at that moment, or perhaps they just need to complete the steps in AID,Inc. properly.

Is this a skillset or mindset issue, or a bit of both? The only way to tell is to ask coaching questions, such as these:

- When you get to the Close, what are you thinking?

- How do you prepare Closing questions?

- How do you define your role as a salesperson when you get to the Close?

- What signs do you look for before you ask for a Closing commitment?

- What trial-closing questions have you found effective if you want to test the waters?

Fear of feedback

A salesperson moves through the AID,Inc. steps smoothly until she reaches Negotiate. One of the decision-makers with a Supporter behavior style expresses reluctance about moving forward. The salesperson tries to offer reassurance, but the decision to buy is put on hold. Later the salesperson approaches her manager and says, "I need to improve my negotiation skills. I was outmaneuvered again."

What happened here? If we could go back in time, the salesperson would see that it wasn't her negotiation skills that failed her. She was so focused on moving ahead to Closing the sale that, somewhere between the Demonstrate and Negotiate steps, she forgot to ask the questions, "Do you have any concerns? Do the benefits I just demonstrated give you the value you are looking for?"

Is this a skillset or mindset issue, or a bit of both? The only way to tell is to ask coaching questions, such as these:

- How do you help your customers discover value in a product?

- What factors might affect your customers' perception of value?

- What clues help you understand how a customer's behavior style might affect action?

- How do you address concerns? Are you comfortable asking for feedback?

- What are your natural tendencies (linked to your behavior style) when a customer disagrees with you?

- Describe how you use the ACR system (acknowledge, clarify, and respond).

Selling at a discount

A sales leader keeps seeing the same pattern. When customers express concerns or hesitancy during a closing step in a sale, some of the salespeople "solve" the problem by offering a discount.

At a weekly check-in, the manager discusses where to increase activity, what products could be added, what product knowledge is missing, and what tactics need to change. She then pulls out a report on pipeline activity and sales revenue for the month to show where each salesperson is falling behind. But no amount of pressure seems to make a difference. The discounts keep coming!

What happened here? It sounds like some of the salespeople have issues with one of the products, and it's getting in the way of their belief in the product. Perhaps there were past failures or service issues or some internal dissonance within the company. Or maybe they need help selling value beyond price.

Is this a skillset or mindset issue, or a bit of both? The only way to tell is to ask coaching questions, such as these:

- Tell me what you think is happening during the Close step.

- What do you think about our products? How do they create value for customers?

- What qualities do you bring as a salesperson?

- Do your values align with the company? Do you feel they need to be in sync?

First, they need to Validate you

A salesperson returns from training, where he's been inspired by what he learned. But a voice inside his head keeps coming up with reasons to avoid putting these new techniques and tools in action. Sometimes the message is, "Wouldn't you rather just meet with a customer you know?" Other times, the voice questions his values—"Am I being too pushy?"—or erodes his confidence—"Maybe I need more practice, more knowledge, a better product, additional support?"

What is happening here? Several lenses in the Sales Congruence Model need alignment here: view of selling, view of abilities, and belief in product. Gaps in these internal beliefs are affecting the salesperson's commitment to activities necessary to increase sales performance. There may also be a gap in understanding how to put the new skills into practice.

Is this a skillset or mindset issue, or a bit of both? The only way to tell is to ask coaching questions, such as these:

- What is your purpose behind why you sell?

- What words best describe your values and ethics? How might you demonstrate these values during the AID,Inc. process?

- What skills would increase your confidence during the Approach and Interview steps?

- How do you translate features into benefits?

Not believing in your salespeople

The sales manager for a distribution company spent several years as a rep before being promoted. She'd always been a high performer and expects the same from the salespeople who now report to her. When sales quotas are missed, she expresses her disappointment to her team by reviewing the sales goals and emphasizing the competitive nature of their industry. Deep down, however, she doesn't think most of them are up to the job.

The manager's reps feel like failures as salespeople. The manager feels like a failure as a sales coach.

What happened here? People tend to perform in a way that's consistent with their inner beliefs. External feedback enhances and solidifies those inner beliefs. The manager's beliefs, therefore, play an equally important role in the effectiveness of any sales coaching conversation. People quickly pick up on whether you believe in them or not. As a result, the manager's attitude directly affects the success of the coaching.

In addition, expanding beliefs isn't just about the mindset of the person being coached. The sales manager struggles because of her lack of coaching abilities, so she has lost confidence in herself as a leader.

Is this a skillset or mindset issue, or a bit of both? The only way to tell is to ask coaching questions, such as these:

- Do I believe in the potential of my team?

- What level of performance do I expect from this team? How can I change that?

- What coaching questions can I prepare ahead of time?

- Where can I get training in effective coaching skills?

The Need for Coaching

Employees who are coached outperform their peers, are significantly more engaged, have more confidence, and apply more discretionary effort.

Coaching also affects the bottom line. Integrity Solutions researched sales coaching in partnership with the Sales Management Association and learned that the revenue performance achievement gap between leading firms that were effective at coaching versus firms seen as ineffective at coaching was 15 percent. Just think of what you could do with another 15 percent of revenue!

When we looked at why companies struggle, we learned that the vast majority—three-quarters of them—left it up to individual managers to define what coaching is and figure it out as they go. There was no common definition or accountability for it. And yet, even with this lack of attention being placed on coaching, 76 percent of the firms in our study said they believe sales coaching is a critical driver of success. The same percentage also admitted they do too little of it. When asked why, time was the biggest reason given, followed by not having any training in coaching. Clearly, companies need help to make coaching part of the culture.

Unlocking Success One Conversation at a Time

Coaching works because it is designed to get to the real problem. As humans, we are imperfect. We can have the best practices in the world (like AID,Inc.!), great technology tools, and training whenever we need it, but sometimes we forget things, sometimes we let our emotions get in the way, sometimes we get rusty, and sometimes new variables change the playing field. Coaching conversations draw out those factors that enable success while helping us see what's getting in the way.

This chapter can't cover all the complexities of coaching. The above examples are only a few scenarios you may encounter in your sales activities. We hope it clarifies what coaching is (and isn't) and provides coaching questions and techniques to use in your sales activities. Even a slight shift to a sales coaching approach can make a difference.

Add your own stories! The magic here lies in the nature of the questions. Is it a case of not doing the job, or is there something else going on that's getting in the way?

Coaching Corner

Power thought

Coaching isn't therapy. It's product development, with you as the product.
CLAIRE TRISTRAM, JOURNALIST

Questions and reflections
The following are some general questions to ask, depending on the outcome of a sales engagement:

A sales engagement went well
What did you like best about that call?

What went well for you?

What might you do differently next time?

The sales engagement didn't produce the intended results
Reflect more on what happened. What might you do differently next time?

What did you think when the customer expressed an objection?

Questions to build skill and will going forward
What part of the process/conversation do you find the most challenging and why?

What can you do to practice a particular skill or expand a belief boundary?

What does a successful outcome look like for you?

Great leaders are always trying to get better. Scan this QR code to take a free coaching assessment.

15

The Emotionally Intelligent Salesperson

OACHING IS about helping people expand beliefs about what they are capable of accomplishing. The coaching examples in the last chapter were designed to help you work through some of the most common problems that managers and salespeople face when it comes to selling. Maybe one or two made you cringe because they hit too close to home. Or perhaps they made you reflect on a past conversation and think, "I wish I had approached that situation differently."

Coaching questions and conversations don't come easily to most of us—whether we are the ones asking the questions or the ones being asked. Learning how to ask sales coaching questions—of yourself or others—takes practice. The big takeaway is that coaching conversations should never sound like, "Let me give you feedback about what you're doing wrong and what you should be doing better. And by the way, here are all your faults."

In any leadership or mentorship role, there's a tendency to become what coaching expert Michael Bungay Stanier calls an "advice monster." It's hard to wait patiently while someone thinks through their solution. Any chance we get, we want to jump in with an answer to a problem. As human beings, we're also wired to resist feedback. Some researchers think this is because, as children, we grow up constantly being told what not to do. As a result, we equate advice with criticism. There's also the fear, both real and imagined, that if we acknowledge the feedback, it could be used against us.

This all brings us to one more set of skills to talk about: emotional intelligence. Coaching, or being coached, requires emotional intelligence in both parties to be effective. As you read through the qualities of an emotionally intelligent person, you'll be able to see why emotional intelligence and success in sales go hand in hand.

Begin by Recognizing Emotional Awareness in Others

There are two attributes most recognizable in those who have high emotional intelligence, also known as EQ:

- The ability to "tune in" to those around you with empathy and understanding—an emotionally intelligent person can read a room well and behave accordingly.

- The ability to recognize and understand your feelings and emotions and the impact of them on your behavior. You also help others do the same.

Emotional intelligence goes hand in hand with our emphasis on the human side of sales. High EQ is critical to successful sales and its related functions, such as customer service. The difference is evident in the person's behavior, conversations, and reactions.

See how a salesperson with high EQ handles each of the following examples.

Example 1: A busy doctor enters the room, obviously distracted by what appears to be some emergency.

The emotionally intelligent salesperson picks up on the cues, puts his own agenda aside, and suggests he return another day. In the meantime, he considers what else he can do while on-site.

Example 2: A customer digs in her heels at the last minute and says she doesn't think your product will be worth the cost.

The emotionally intelligent salesperson feels frustrated but pauses a few seconds before calmly asking for clarification. When the meeting ends without a sale, she puts her disappointment behind her and thinks about ways of keeping the relationship strong despite the setback.

Example 3: A sales manager attends a meeting where he expects a sale to close, but the salesperson never asks directly for the business.

In a Coaching Moment following the meeting, the emotionally intelligent sales manager calmly asks the salesperson to talk about what happened and why. He believes in her potential and listens empathetically when she explains her hesitancy. As they talk, the salesperson and the manager begin to see how gaps in congruence are getting in the way of success.

Example 4: A salesperson wants to take time off to attend a friend's funeral, but his call reports are due that day.

Empathy is a core component of EQ. The emotionally intelligent manager forgets the numbers for a day and takes care of the salesperson. She expresses concern for him and assures him that someone else will cover the work while he's gone.

The Surprising Success of High EQ

There was a time when most people assumed that successful careers were founded on expertise (hard skills) in a technical, functional, or professional domain. However, research over the past few decades has found that soft skills such as communication and the ability to show empathy are far more powerful than anyone had previously believed.

Scientist and writer Daniel Goleman was one of the first to introduce the idea of emotional intelligence. Goleman's work and research have shown that EQ is twice as important as IQ (combined with technical skills) for determining career success.

It's not hard to see how coaching, emotional intelligence, and sales work so well together when it comes to selling with integrity.

Salespeople who develop emotional intelligence skills build trusted relationships with customers and colleagues more effectively. Customers believe in them and the value they are delivering. All of this feeds the salesperson's level of confidence and success.

EQ and Sales

The attributes of emotional intelligence are organized under four categories: self-awareness, self-management, social awareness, and relationship management. Entire books have been written about how to apply these attributes in life and business. Here are a few ways to look at the four from a sales point of view and consider how they affect you as a salesperson.

Self-awareness means being honest about what you're feeling and the impact your emotions may have on your actions and on others. For example, when you have excellent self-awareness

- you can answer questions such as, "What happened during that failed sales call?" and you can also analyze what caused a call to go well so you know how to duplicate it the next time;

- you welcome feedback because it helps you understand which influences are getting in the way of you doing the activities; and

- you bounce back better after a rejection because you recognize the negative feelings but don't let them drag you down.

Self-management is about impulse control. We all recognize this one. Someone says something annoying, and you have the good sense (high EQ) to count to six and then respond calmly and politely. For example, when you have good self-management

- you can handle meetings when customers state objections or start back-pedaling about a decision;

- you see challenges as opportunities and know that how you respond to others can change the outcome;

- you embrace ACR (acknowledge, clarify, respond) as a helpful tool to use before reacting to objections; and

- you recognize that when you're having a bad day or not getting along with your boss, you may need to take a break before engaging with customers.

Within self-management is the drive to achieve, or "motivation," which we discussed in Chapter 1. It's the subconscious force that pushes us to work toward our goals. With motivation

- you get more done in a day than most and, over time, meet your goals;

- you have a purpose for what you do, which gives you energy and focus; and

- you have a "growth mindset" versus a "fixed mindset." You believe learning is a lifelong activity and that even the most experienced professionals always try to improve. (We'll discuss a growth mindset in Chapter 16.)

Social awareness is the ability to accurately notice the emotions of others and "read" situations appropriately. It is about sensing what other people are thinking and feeling to be able to take their perspective using your capacity for empathy. Empathy is the cornerstone of the social skills domain. With empathy

- you listen well because you are sincerely curious about your customers;

- you can read a room and pick up on signals, so you sense immediately when it's not a good time to talk to someone; and

- you pay attention to Behavior Styles and know the best way to engage people in the conversation. You can tell by the tone of voice or the circumstance when a customer ceases to be engaged.

Relationship management is about getting along well with others. What's important to remember is that you don't have to be an extrovert to have good people skills. You do, however, need good people skills to be emotionally intelligent. When you have strong relationship management skills

- you are able to influence those around you to make a good decision;

- you show genuine interest in your customers and demonstrate this by being authentic and actively listening;

- you can sense others' reactions to a situation (conflict) and fine-tune your response to move the interaction in a positive direction;

- you build trust with your customers, communicate clearly, collaborate well, and act with integrity throughout the sales process; and

- you welcome feedback and view objections as a way to strengthen relationships.

Can I Increase My Emotional Intelligence?

Some people have a higher EQ than others. But experts say that EQ skills can be taught, which is good news for all of us. Many resources are available, such as communication workshops that include EQ as part of the training. There also are steps you can take to work on gaining greater EQ on your own. For instance:

- Take a moment before each sales engagement to recognize your strengths and be realistic about what might be a challenge for you in this situation.

- Keep detailed pre- and post-call notes and review them on your own or with your sales manager. Perhaps you acted defensively during a sales interaction when a customer objected. Or you successfully picked up on their behavior style and moved the conversation to the next step. What can you learn from these occasions?

- Willingly accept coaching to improve your sales or management skills, even if you have years of experience as a salesperson or leader.

- Invest in communication and EQ skills training.

- If you're a manager, when a rep comes to you about not hitting their goal, most of the time they just need to talk it through with someone—and all you need to do is listen.

Coaching Corner

Power thought

Emotionally intelligent people... learn from their mistakes, and they learn from their triumphs, and they're always changing themselves for the better.
DR. TRAVIS BRADBERRY, AUTHOR OF *EMOTIONAL INTELLIGENCE HABITS*

Questions and reflections

Various emotional intelligence assessments are available. Use this quick assessment as a first step. Rate yourself from 1 to 10 on each of the following (1 is low EQ and 10 is high):

- Active listener and genuinely interested in others

- Excellent at reading body language, tone of voice, and facial expressions

- Get along with others

- Self-confident but not afraid of constructive criticism and feedback

- Know my strengths and weaknesses

- Conscientious, trustworthy, and act with integrity

- Self-control over emotions; I can observe emotions in a detached way and identify why I'm upset

- Strong achievement drive (self-motivated)

- Good awareness of boundaries; I know my limits and what is possible given my time and energy

- Optimistic and focused on the present, not what went wrong

EQ is particularly powerful when meeting objections. Think of a time when someone responded with an objection or you began to see a potential sale slipping away. Rate yourself on your

- ability to understand your emotions and know that you would feel disappointment and perhaps frustration;

- willingness to show patience and think of ways to keep the relationship moving forward;

- ability to remain poised and under control during a stressful situation, listen, and then accept that the customer wasn't ready to take positive action at the time; and

- resilience to bounce back after the rejection and not let it affect your belief in your abilities.

16

Self and Team
Assessments

BERNIE HAD A stellar career in sales. He traveled the country meeting customers face-to-face, shaking their hands, and looking them directly in the eyes with a big smile and a hearty "How are you doing?" He could remember every detail about his customers, not just the products they liked but also the names of their kids and their favorite vacation spots. "I can always make a sale," he'd tell his team. "Just give me enough time over a meal or on the golf course, and I'll close the sale."

Everyone figured that Bernie was an expert at sales—that is, until selling was forced to go virtual and no one was able to meet clients in person. Bernie was so convinced that virtual wouldn't work that he didn't even try to learn the technology. He waited so long for face-to-face selling to return to how it used to be that... well, he's still waiting.

. . . .

WE THINK OF an expert as someone with specific abilities or extensive knowledge. But, over time, a new technology comes along, markets evolve, and circumstances change. An expert mechanic isn't that helpful if their skillset is based on a Studebaker.

True professionals know they are good, understand why they are good, and always try to get better. You may possess all the expertise in the world, but expertise alone is not enough if you don't continue to add to your knowledge and overall competency, especially in an environment that's changing as fast as ours is. Continually learning about new trends and acquiring new skills will improve both your ability to perform and the value you bring to your customers.

Growth Mindset: There's Always Room for Improvement

We now return to the self-imposed beliefs from the Sales Congruence Model that influence the conversation in your head when you're selling. If your view of your abilities is low, your confidence when it comes to learning will be, too. Shifting your beliefs toward a growth mindset improves your view.

When you have a growth mindset, learning or exploring something new triggers positive emotions. These, in turn, give you greater confidence. You continually seek to learn more and improve, even when you've reached a high level of expertise and professionalism in your field.

Do You Have a Growth or Fixed Mindset?

The following examples illustrate the difference between a growth mindset and a fixed mindset. What is the conversation in your head? What do you need to help you make the shift?

Fixed mindset: I'm either naturally good at something or I'm not.

Growth mindset: I can improve my skills with training and practice.

Fixed mindset: When people give me feedback, it feels like criticism.

Growth mindset: I appreciate it when people give me feedback. It helps me get better at what I do.

Fixed mindset: I'm already really good at sales. I don't need to get any better.

Growth mindset: There's always room for improvement.

Self-Assessments and Performance Assessments

We can all use a little help with a growth mindset. You may not need a coach if you know how to self-assess using coaching questions. However, most of us don't see our blind spots. Or we know what to do, but we need help staying consistent.

These are the times when we need someone to be what golfers call a "swing coach." This is someone who typically looks at small movements or changes that can make a big difference in a person's overall play and offers incisive comments like, "Hey, you're dipping your shoulder right here, and that's why you're slicing the ball."

Consider finding an outside coach who can help you in a similar manner. Remember the five dimensions in the Sales Congruence Model: Often just a slight adjustment can make a world of difference in how you view yourself or your abilities.

A coach is someone who can encourage you to do the right things, even when it is just a small adjustment. You become aware of what you're doing and why, you improve your ability to prioritize, and you learn how to assess your progress.

Continue to Grow in the Right Ways

You've learned ways to listen and talk to yourself and others, and you've learned the basics of coaching conversations with others and yourself in order to ensure your ongoing development in these skills. You've no doubt had lots of experience with performance management techniques, as someone on the receiving end and, perhaps, as a manager helping salespeople stay productive.

Use the tools in this chapter to assess your performance. This is an important part of developing a growth mindset through conversations with yourself, your manager, and your salespeople. These tools assess the use of AID,Inc., the Sales Congruence Model, and how you deliver value. Implied in each assessment are skills related to emotional intelligence.

- If you are a salesperson, use each tool to identify areas where you need help and to track progress. Set goals for yourself in areas that need strengthening. There may be areas where you need support through additional coaching and training.

- If you are a sales manager, use these assessments to challenge your people to grow in their skills; improve their views of selling, their abilities, and the product; and improve their commitment to activities. Remember, your team will perform at a higher level when you believe in their potential. Coach to the behaviors and skills of

AID,Inc. and the Sales Congruence Model, and you'll open a world of possibilities.

Do sales managers need self-assessment and coaching? You bet! In addition to outside expertise, these practices help develop your skills in sales coaching and leadership. For example, sales leaders at Integrity Solutions use the assessments in this chapter weekly to check on how well they are doing. Even the best of the best sometimes skips a step in AID,Inc. or lets an emotional response influence the outcome of a meeting.

Coaching to the Sales Congruence Model

Make it a weekly practice to assess yourself or your salespeople on the Sales Congruence Model to identify gaps and assess alignment. Rate yourself from 1 (low) to 10 (high) on the model's five areas:

1 View of selling

2 View of abilities

3 Values

4 Commitment to activities

5 Belief in product

To self-assess or to use this assessment as a sales manager, ask these questions:

- What makes you most passionate about sales?

- How do you describe what you do to friends and family?

- Do you believe you have the ability to be successful?

- Do you live by and model values of integrity, honesty, and sincerity?

- Are you willing to do all the activities required to be a successful salesperson?

- How strongly do you believe your products and services create value for customers?

- Do you have an unwavering belief in your potential?

- What action steps might you take to break through a limiting belief?

- What keeps you from trying something outside your comfort zone?

- How have you overcome barriers in the past?

- Think about a time you failed in the past that you now realize was a great learning experience. How can you shift the conversation in your head so your behavior helps instead of limits success?

Tips for using this assessment:

- The goal is to assess your strengths and note the gaps honestly. These are the "influencers" that impact your job satisfaction and the performance of your team. They may change over time. They'll even vary depending on the kind of week you've had. If you've ever tried to close a sale after a major account turned you down, you likely know what we mean. However, if there is a pattern to what you see, set goals with specific actions to bring each of the five areas into alignment.

- Suggest one or two actions to build belief, set a goal, and agree on how you will stay accountable to each goal.

- Each week, review the assessment and note what has changed and why.

- Make sure you mark each assessment with a date so you can compare them over time.

- Look beyond the symptom. When someone isn't doing the necessary activities, it's likely related to one or more of the other four dimensions. Instructing the salesperson repeatedly to do these activities isn't going to work. Questions that get to the real heart of the matter could include, "How did you get into sales?" and "Why do you hesitate to ask questions?"

- Ask questions with curiosity, not judgment. "You didn't talk about this particular product. Is there a reason?"

- Give praise when a salesperson has success. Provide assurance that their goals are possible and you believe they deserve to achieve them.

The AID,Inc. General Assessment

As with the Sales Congruence Model assessment, use the following questions to assess how well you use AID,Inc. as a sales process, and identify what might help you use it with greater results.

- What have you found most challenging about applying the process?

- What element(s) of AID,Inc. do you think you do best?

- What is one area in which you'd like to strengthen your skills?

- What additional training would be helpful?

- How will you adapt AID,Inc. when communicating with customers by phone, video, text, or email?

The AID,Inc. Step-by-Step Assessment

Ideally, you will do this assessment following a recent call. Review the model and rate yourself on your completed steps using a scale of 1 to 5, with 1 being not at all and 5 being excellent. Ask yourself how well you did the following:

Approach
- Establish rapport with people
- Identify and adjust to Behavior Styles
- Focus and listen well
- Make an excellent first impression

Interview
- Ask meaningful, appropriate questions
- Focus on understanding needs first before demonstrating product
- Notice my customer's behavior style
- Phrase questions differently according to my customer's style and my own style
- Listen (rather than talk) 80 percent of the time

Demonstrate

- Present information that appeals to the behavior style of the customer
- Continually ask for feedback during and after the demonstration
- Talk in terms of end-result benefits for customer's customers

Validate

- Communicate honestly and sincerely
- Give evidence to back up product claims
- Speak to the integrity of my organization

Negotiate

- Listen to and work through customer's concerns
- Deal with problems or roadblocks calmly and skillfully
- Use ACR (acknowledge, clarify, respond)

Close

- Intuitively know when to ask for decisions or commitments
- Clarify incremental Closes that lead to a buying decision
- Ask for action—without fear—when I believe it to be in the customer's best interests

Tips for Using the AID,Inc. Assessment

Keep it simple. What did you notice in the call? What went well, and what got missed?

To strengthen skills and build belief, pick one area that needs improvement, not several. When someone is conceding on price every time, that's a red flag. Ask, "What's going on? Why do you think this happens?"

After a sale has been made, do a debrief:

- What led to an action on the customer's part? Why do you think this was the case?

Also debrief after a meeting where little or no progress was made:

- Would you do anything differently another time? What else might you have asked?

- What did you notice about the decision-makers, what style do you think they might be, and how might you phrase your questions next time?

- What might you record in your pre-call notes for next time?

Customer Experience Assessment: Did You Deliver Value?

The value you bring can be measured in ways that build lasting relationships with your customers. The following questions combine both skillset and mindset. Use them after any sales engagement.

- Did I ask the right questions?

- Did I make the customer's decision process more effective?

- Did I listen well and provide solutions that are specifically relevant to their needs?

- Did I respect and adapt to the way my customers want to make a purchasing decision?

- Did I do the right thing for the customer, including walking away if it was not the right match or was the right thing to do?

- Did I make this an exceptional experience for the customer?

- Did my customer return to their colleagues and say, "Hey, that was easy, even delightful"?

Don't Forget Your Superstars!

Savvy sales managers help their top performers grow rather than assume they're doing fine and leave them alone.

Silvia, for instance, was the best performer on her team. She met or exceeded her quota each quarter, and her customers were loyal. The best part about managing Silvia was that it took no effort. Her manager left her alone and focused on others who created challenges.

As a result, Silvia had no idea she was such a valued employee. All she saw was that everyone else got the attention, including additional training options and one-on-one time with the manager. The harder she worked, the more alone she felt. Burned out and frustrated by the lack of new opportunities, she left for another job. Her sales manager was stunned. What had happened?

The best players want to work for the best coaches in sports. No one can afford to ignore their best people. It's a misconception that can lead to burnout, plateauing, and turnover. The Silvias of the world are the ones who should be getting the most coaching!

Coaching Corner

Power thought

*Consistently and overwhelmingly, the evidence
showed that experts are always made, not born.*
K. ANDERS ERICSSON, MICHAEL J. PRIETULA,
AND EDWARD T. COKELY, RESEARCHERS

Questions and reflections

Part of developing a growth mindset is taking time to recognize
your achievements and celebrate successes.

What are some areas where you have strengthened your skills?
What difference did this make in other areas, such as building
relationships? Asking smart questions? Closing a sale?

Think about a specific sale you made or a customer relationship you improved. What makes you particularly proud of these
achievements?

Looking back over the year so far, you'll see some patterns.
Consider creating a "keep-doing, stop-doing" list to recalibrate
your thinking, adjust your growth mindset, and set some learning priorities.

What are your learning goals for the next three months, six
months, and year? What can you put in place to ensure you
act on these goals?

Conclusion: Choosing to Deliver a Different Selling Experience

THINK ABOUT your last social gathering. When you told people "I'm in sales," did their eyes roll? Or did you find another way to describe what you do?

Start with your business card. What does it say? We often meet salespeople who say they are proud to be in sales, but when you look at their business card, it reads "Account Manager," "Relationship Manager," or "Customer Development." What's going on here?

It's time to own the role and say, "I'm a salesperson and I'm proud of it!"

Every company that sells a product or service looks for ways to define its difference. As we noted at the beginning of this book, when two products solve the same problem and cost the same, this can be a challenge. Product differentiation is only the tip of the iceberg. As a salesperson, you are lumped into the same category as every other salesperson. On their own, all the training, skills, and confidence in the world aren't going to make you stand out in the crowd.

What if there was a way to define differentiation throughout the buying journey? And what if this difference resonated with your customers on a much more meaningful level than how well you recite your products' features or master the latest technology tools?

There is one last conversation we need to consider: What's going on inside a customer's head when they go through the sales process with *you*?

What Do Customers Want?

Annual surveys tell us that everyone wants a positive customer experience. Definitions of what that means vary, but at the core, customers don't want to "be sold."

What Customers Want

Knowledge with wisdom versus dumping and overwhelming
Respect versus making you feel like you've got it all wrong
Ease versus friction and pressure
Authenticity versus slick, high-pressure sales
Listening versus talking and assuming

Our research, based on over fifty years in the sales training industry, supports these findings. The ideal customer experience is one in which the salesperson enables a decision through an interaction that feels easy, even enjoyable, and there's an optimal outcome on both sides. Both the customer and the salesperson benefit.

- The customer feels good about their decision. They're satisfied with how much they learned before making a purchase. Their problem has been solved.

- The salesperson is confident about their role in the process, the knowledge they provided, and how well they've enabled helpful discussion and decision-making. They've built trust and loyalty by establishing themselves as a valuable resource. The conversations that took place can now become a catalyst for an ongoing partnership with the company.

- No one (particularly the customer!) feels manipulated, pressured, annoyed, defensive, or misunderstood.

- Both walk away thinking, "Wow, that was a positive sales experience."

Values-Based Selling

An ideal sales experience like that results from what we refer to as values-based selling. Values-based selling resonates with people. It's not the products, the price, or "the deal" you put together. The key ingredients you bring are your values.

These values put the customer first and are the same values you would never compromise in the sales experience. They affect everything you do, including the way you treat people, how you approach the selling engagement, and the priority you place on customer needs versus your own.

When you approach selling from this values-based perspective, you give off unconscious signals to the customer. Rapport increases, along with trust, loyalty, and the potential for a long-term relationship—all of which keep the customer-first brand of your organization strong.

Redefining the Difference You Bring

Not only do your values differentiate the customer experience, but they also make you confident and proud of what you do. And when *you are the difference*, your view of selling shifts. You know, without a doubt, what you are doing is mutually valuable, and the way you sell is ethical and affirming. That sense of "bothering people" or "being slick" has disappeared. It's replaced by confidence and a purpose fueled by an unstoppable achievement drive.

Having strong values and being successful in sales go hand in hand. You do all the right things to sell effectively and, in the process, make a lot more money.

Aligning Selling Culture with Core Values

A large financial institution came to us at Integrity Solutions because they wanted to enhance their culture. Both *selling* and *coaching* had a negative connotation, and they needed to clarify how sales aligned with their overall core values.

Training and implementation of a values-based sales program took a year. It included programs that combined mindset and skillset to build confidence in abilities and confirm how each contributed to the organization's success. The sales team learned how to create value for customers by listening to them and confidently identifying their needs, offering the appropriate products or services to meet them, and adding value to the relationship. Coaching also had a major impact on how employees understood each other and worked together daily.

The sales team's successes were tracked since the program's implementation, and the results speak for themselves:

increased employee satisfaction, reduced turnover, and improved collaboration across departments, in addition to more deposits and loans.

The Integrity Selling Values and Ethics: Doing the Right Thing Is the Right Thing to Do. Period.

Values and ethics are non-negotiable. They are the right way to sell; they also are the most effective way to fulfill the purpose you've defined for yourself.

Five key values and ethics for success in sales are listed below. After each is an explanation of how these translate into the sales experience. They should all sound familiar to you because they reflect what you've read throughout this book.

Truth, respect, and honesty provide the basis for long-term selling success

Truth, respect, and honesty don't just happen; they must be earned before any selling activity begins. They are part of your overall mindset about selling going into a sales engagement, and they are demonstrated at every step of the sales process.

When you see yourself as someone who's there to serve the customer rather than make a sale, you take time to listen and understand before making assumptions or pushing for a decision. In return, clients trust you as a resource, value your knowledge, and, as the engagement deepens, believe you will be straightforward and honest in every conversation.

Selling isn't something you do to people; it's something you do for and with them

When selling is done "to them," customers quickly sense it, perhaps in the way you discredit their choice or try to get them to decide before they are ready. However, when selling is done "for and with them," the result is a low-friction, even enjoyable engagement.

Selling "for and with" people is something you do because you genuinely care for your customers. Such care is shown when you take time to listen, understand, and learn about your client's business. Care is also demonstrated through emotional intelligence skills such as patience and understanding. You aren't defensive just because they need time to wrestle with a decision. The only pressure applied is pressure by the customer when they realize they want your products or services.

Understanding wants or needs must always precede any attempt to sell

Values and ethics contribute to sales success more than techniques or strategies. Too many salespeople demonstrate their product knowledge and their own expertise before letting the client talk about what they want and what they are experiencing.

When you have your customers' best interests in mind, your job is about understanding wants and needs, not selling stuff or dumping out choices. The only way to do so is to listen. You'll learn more and, as a result, be able to ask smart questions. Your customers will know you've taken the time to step into their world and truly work with them.

Negotiation is never manipulation

In values-based selling, negotiation is a strategy for both parties to work through concerns together.

There's always a negotiation aspect to the sales process, but customers should never feel like they've been misled or backed into a corner. Your internal ethics would never cause you to manipulate a decision or sell in a misleading way.

As a salesperson, you demonstrate strong negotiation skills when your values are based on wanting to listen, understand, and help, not on closing the sale.

Well-thought-out, high-impact questions, for example, help a client reframe something or think about a solution differently. Product knowledge and insight add value to a discussion. Presenting choices helps reframe a need. Good preparation helps put their minds at ease when they have concerns or questions.

Closing is everybody's victory

Closing the sale is a victory for everyone involved.

Closing should deliver a mutual exchange of value. You know this happens when you and your customer leave feeling good about the experience. Not only have you successfully sold a product, but you've also done so in a way that aligns with your values. Your customer has a product that fits their needs. They've also built a trusted partnership with someone who is honest, ethical, and going to be there for them long after the sale has closed.

What Does the Conversation in Your Head Tell You Now?

Let's return to what is on your business card. As a salesperson, you have much more influence on your success than you may realize. Are you ready to be proud of who you are?

Change has happened in the sales industry and will continue to happen. You have no choice but to embrace it. But what doesn't change is your power to act with integrity. This principle will remain true as long as humans sell to humans.

With all the emotion and personality that comes with them, these human elements influence the conversations people have with customers, managers, and sales professionals, as well as the conversations in their heads. Maybe you've told yourself, "I'm just not going to succeed in this market." If that's what you believe, no amount of skills training or pressure from above will make a difference in your performance.

And if you've ever said to yourself, "Salespeople aren't necessary anymore," hopefully this book has changed your perspective. Now more than ever, there is value in the sales professional. Computers can't replace you. Just because your customers are being inundated with mountains of information, it doesn't mean they're better able to make well-informed or high-value decisions. They're also crying out for human interaction with trusted, values-driven salespeople who listen to them and work with them, not sell at them. The world needs you.

Every step in the sales process is an opportunity for you in your sales role to choose the x-factor that makes you stand out from your competition. You'll meet your goals by aligning your self-beliefs and embracing tools and techniques from coaching to build self-awareness and emotional intelligence. You'll demonstrate values-based selling in how you move through the AID,Inc. process. You'll show care in the disciplined ways you prepare for sales engagements and create meaningful conversations by listening to sell.

And that's not all. You will gain confidence from believing in yourself. You will be secure in knowing you have what it takes to deal with whatever challenges or setbacks come your way.

Do you hear that? Doors are unlocking for you. Get ready for a new level of success.

Coaching Corner

Power thought

Living into our values means that we do more than profess our values, we practice them.
BRENÉ BROWN, RESEARCHER AND AUTHOR

Questions and reflections

Look at the Integrity Selling Values and Ethics in the Appendix. Add examples of how you live out these values with your customers.

What's on your business card?

How many sales have you closed this year? How many customers have committed to taking the next step in the sales process with you? Celebrate the impact you are having on customers, in addition to your numbers.

What have you learned from reading this book?

What has inspired you? What has made you feel proud of being in sales?

Acknowledgments

A COMPLETE list of thank yous could fill another chapter. Some of the people and organizations who deserve special recognition include:

- Ron Willingham, who was a pioneer in developing customer-focused selling.

- Our global sales team who applied these selling principles to acquire new clients.

- Thousands of companies from six continents that trusted us, reshaped their sales cultures, and achieved stellar results.

- Millions of individual salespeople who lived these concepts, impacted their customers, and changed the perception of sales.

- Hundreds of Integrity Solutions and client facilitators who spread these values-oriented messages.

- Will Milano and Steve Barry, who encouraged us to write this book.

- Steve deBree, Mike Fisher, Bruce Wedderburn, Steve Schmidt, Julie ann Wessinger, Steven Lozada, and many others who contributed stories.

- Beth Parker, who was a world-class master at pulling together this comprehensive manuscript.

- The creative Page Two team that crafted a campaign to take this book to market.

- Marla Lepore, Robyn Doty, Blake Esterday, and others who proofed and refined the message.

- All of the dedicated Integrity Solutions team members who supported us and our clients to make a positive impact.

- Our wives, Terry Esterday and Amy Roberts, and our children, who have put up with so many late nights and days away from home.

Thank you to everyone who reads this book. Our wish is that by applying these proven ideas, your professional and personal dreams will come true!

Appendix

Integrity Selling® Values and Ethics

1 Selling is a mutual exchange of value.

2 Selling isn't something you do to people; it's something you do for and with them.

3 Develop trust and rapport before any selling activity begins.

4 Understanding wants or needs must always precede any attempt to sell.

5 Selling techniques give way to values-driven principles.

6 Truth, respect, and honesty provide the basis for long-term selling success.

7 Ethics and values contribute more to sales success than techniques or strategies.

8 Selling pressure is never exerted by a sales professional. It's exerted only by customers when they recognize they want your solution.

9 Negotiation is never manipulation. It's a strategy to work through concerns—when customers want to work through them.

10 Closing is a victory for the customer and the sales professional.

Behavior Styles® Checklist

Select one description from each row that best fits the person being assessed.

Personality	☐ Outgoing	☐ Dominating
Environment	☐ Cluttered/Pictures	☐ Trophies/Awards
Personal Style	☐ People-oriented	☐ Results-oriented
Responsiveness	☐ Friendly/Affable	☐ Impatient/Restless
Listening	☐ Drifting	☐ Impatient
Talking	☐ About people	☐ About achievement
Relations	☐ Empathizes with others	☐ Directs others
Decisiveness	☐ Popular/Emotional	☐ Quick/Impulsive
Time Usage	☐ Socializes at expense of time	☐ Always pushed for time
Pace	☐ Enthusiastic	☐ Fast
Voice	☐ Emotional/Animated	☐ Emotional/Direct
Gestures	☐ Open	☐ Impatient
Dress	☐ Stylish	☐ Formal
Manner	☐ Friendly	☐ Dominating
Conversation	☐ People	☐ Bottom line
TOTAL	__ Talker	__ Doer

Name:

_____

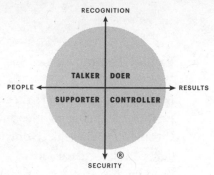

RECOGNITION

TALKER | DOER

PEOPLE ← | → RESULTS

SUPPORTER | CONTROLLER

® SECURITY

☐ Easygoing	☐ No-nonsense
☐ Keepsakes/Relics	☐ Order/Charts
☐ Process-oriented	☐ Facts-oriented
☐ Steady/Reserved	☐ Cool/Distant
☐ Willing	☐ Selective
☐ About functions	☐ About organization
☐ Accepts others	☐ Assesses others
☐ Slow/Studied	☐ Objective/Fact-based
☐ Respects time but not pushed	☐ Values and manages time well
☐ Steady	☐ Controlled
☐ Unemotional/ Low-keyed	☐ Unemotional/ Reserved
☐ Measured	☐ Closed
☐ Conforming	☐ Conservative
☐ Accepting	☐ Evaluating
☐ Systems	☐ Facts
__ **Supporter**	__ **Controller**

Virtual Meeting Tips

Much of our hesitation in regard to technology is connected to our belief in our abilities and how that affects our mindset. If you don't believe deep down that you have what it takes to succeed in a virtual setting, you could face some powerful headwinds.

Keep in mind that the greatest challenge in virtual meetings is keeping everyone engaged so they forget they are separated by a screen. The following tips may help you to break that virtual wall and increase your confidence when meeting online:

- Don't keep the guests a mystery. As the meeting host, introduce everyone at the beginning and stop to introduce those who join late. If someone leaves the meeting, inform the group.

- If you can, request that everyone appear on camera. Doing so cuts down on the amount of multitasking that often takes place. It also increases engagement rates.

- Remember, the principles of AID,Inc. still apply in virtual sales meetings. Virtual meetings are conversations, not "presentations." No one wants to sit through a lecture or someone reciting the slides of a PowerPoint deck.

- Keep your energy level high and keep the meeting moving along. A set agenda and closing time are essential.

- Use various tools to add interest, such as screen share, short videos, and interactive placeholder slides to solicit feedback. Make sure you can confidently share a screen and do a virtual hand-off.

- Thoughtful questions that keep the conversation focused on the customer are particularly important. A decision-maker is less likely to get distracted when talking about themselves!

- To compensate for the fact that you're not there in person, send visual cues that you are listening intently. Nod, lean in, and ensure you look into the camera and smile when appropriate. Use hand gestures (which is why a computer is preferable to a phone).

- It's easy to get lost in a virtual group. Don't let one or two individuals dominate. Seek input from everyone by asking directly, "Sally, what do you think?"

- Chat boxes are a way to extend the conversation to everyone. Depending on the group size, assign a colleague to facilitate the questions.

- Respect "virtual etiquette," a term applied to the professionalism everyone should expect on a screen. Dress appropriately, do not eat or drink while on video, and avoid visual distractions in the background.

GAP Analysis Questions

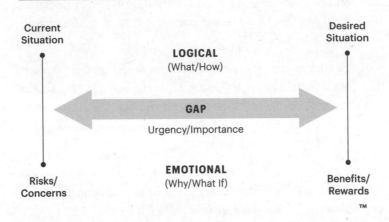

Current situation questions: Where are you now?

- What are you currently using to...?
- What are you currently experiencing with...?
- What challenges or problems are you facing/experiencing?

What does the current situation look like, sound like, feel like?

Desired situation questions: Where would you like to be?

- What outcomes would you like to see?
- If you were to make significant improvements, what would be different?
- What would you like to be doing that currently is difficult or challenging?

What does the desired situation look like, sound like, feel like?

Risks/concerns questions: What are the risks of remaining in the current situation?

- What concerns you about continuing your current approach?
- What risks are you looking to eliminate or reduce?
- What might be the cost over time of staying on the current path?

What is the potential risk or implications of the status quo?

Benefits/rewards questions: How would your life be better if you made a change?

- If you could make the improvements you mentioned, how would that help you?
- Making the adjustments you just suggested, how would things be better?

What would be the benefit of being in the desired situation?

Urgency/importance: How important is it to move toward the desired situation?

- Where does this fit in terms of your priorities?
- How important is it for you to make improvements in this area reasonably quickly?

Is it so important that action should be taken soon?

Notes

Introduction

p. 10   *Buyers crave trust:* Ian Bruce, "Closing the B2B Trust Gap,"
         Forrester Research (blog), November 11, 2021, forrester.com/
         blogs/closing-the-b2b-trust-gap.

p. 10   *LinkedIn research on B2B sales strategies and trends:* Sean Callahan,
         "These 7 Stats Shed Light on the Future of Sales," LinkedIn
         Sales Blog, September 22, 2020, linkedin.com/business/sales/
         blog/b2b-sales/these-7-stats-shed-light-on-the-future-of-sales.

p. 12   *The essence of what scientists have uncovered:* Carol S. Dweck,
         Mindset: The New Psychology of Success (New York: Random
         House, 2006), 5.

p. 14   *My good thoughts are powerful:* Oliver Brown, "Serena Shows
         Strength to Win," *Telegraph*, July 3, 2007, telegraph.co.uk/
         sport/tennis/wimbledon/2316311/Serena-shows-strength
         -to-win.html.

Chapter 1: Establishing Purpose

p. 19   *Fans of* SpongeBob SquarePants: *SpongeBob SquarePants*, season
         3, episode 2, "Club SpongeBob"/"My Pretty Seahorse," created
         by Stephen Hillenburg, aired July 12, 2002, on Nickelodeon.

p. 19   *It's what gives "nobility":* Hemantha Kulathunga, "Selling,
         a Noble Profession," *Sunday Observer* (Sri Lanka), August 2,
         2020, sundayobserver.lk/2020/08/02/business/selling-noble
         -profession.

p. 20   *Companies that put purpose at the core of their strategy:* Thomas W.
         Malnight, Ivy Buche, and Charles Dhanaraj, "Put Purpose at

the Core of Your Strategy," World Forum Disrupt, September 19, 2019, worldforumdisrupt.com/strategy-innovation-london-2020/put-purpose-at-the-core-of-your-strategy.

p. 23   *Don't let anyone tell you:* Lisa Earle McLeod with Elizabeth Lotardo, *Selling with Noble Purpose: How to Drive Revenue and Do Work That Makes You Proud*, 2nd ed. (Hoboken, NJ: John Wiley & Sons, 2020), jacket copy.

Chapter 2: Internal Beliefs

p. 37   *Salespeople are the most important people:* Geoffrey James, "Interview with Chris Gardner ('Pursuit of Happyness')," CBS News, December 23, 2009, cbsnews.com/news/interview-with-chris-gardner-pursuit-of-happyness.

Chapter 3: Getting in Sync

p. 48   *I'm not the next Usain Bolt:* Gabrielle McMillen, "Rio Olympics 2016: Simone Biles Cements Golden Legacy: 'I've Finally Done It,'" *Sporting News*, August 11, 2016, sportingnews.com/us/athletics/news/rio-olympics-2016-simone-biles-all-around-gold-individual-medal-final-five/1x4a8qszafvoo1jb5bjtn3i9oq.

Chapter 4: Communicating Human to Human

p. 51   *In Ned's words: Groundhog Day*, directed by Harold Ramis (Los Angeles, CA: Columbia Pictures, 1993).

p. 52   *One report puts the preference:* Kelly Blum, "Gartner Keynote: B2B Sales Must Focus on Seller-Assisted Digital Experiences," Gartner, May 17, 2021, gartner.com/smarterwithgartner/b2b-sales-must-focus-on-seller-assisted-digital-experiences.

p. 52   *As one researcher on the subject reports:* Hana Benkirane, "Manufacturing Sellers: Become Part of the Value Chain," LinkedIn Sales Blog, June 22, 2021, linkedin.com/business/sales/blog/modern-selling/manufacturing-sellers-become-part-of-the-value-chain.

p. 53   *Recent Gartner research highlights:* "New B2B Buying Journey and Its Implications for Sales," Gartner, 2019, gartner.ca/en/sales/insights/b2b-buying-journey.

p. 63   *If you want to interact effectively:* Stephen R. Covey, *The 7 Habits of Highly Effective People: Powerful Lessons in Personal Change* (New York: Free Press, 2004), 238.

Chapter 5: The AID,Inc. Sales Process

p. 73   *The way you treat people:* Brian Tracy, *Full Engagement! Inspire,
Motivate, and Bring Out the Best in Your People* (New York:
AMACOM, 2011), 6.

Chapter 6: Approaching to Establish Rapport

p. 78   *When people talk about themselves:* Adrian F. Ward, "The
Neuroscience of Everybody's Favorite Topic," *Scientific
American*, July 16, 2013, scientificamerican.com/article/
the-neuroscience-of-everybody-favorite-topic-themselves.

p. 81   *You may have about seven seconds:* Serenity Gibbons, "You and
Your Business Have 7 Seconds to Make a First Impression:
Here's How to Succeed," *Forbes*, June 19, 2018, forbes.com/
sites/serenitygibbons/2018/06/19/you-have-7-seconds-to
-make-a-first-impression-heres-how-to-succeed; Eric Wargo,
"How Many Seconds to a First Impression?" *Observer*
(Association for Psychological Science), July 1, 2006,
psychologicalscience.org/observer/how-many-seconds
-to-a-first-impression.

p. 82   *The old aphorisms are basically sound:* Jessie Redmon Fauset,
Comedy: American Style, ed. Cherene Sherrard-Johnson (New
Brunswick, NJ: Rutgers University Press, 2010), 71.

Chapter 7: Interviewing to Identify
Needs, Challenges, and Goals

p. 93   *Nobody is more persuasive:* Dale Carnegie & Associates, Inc.,
Michael A. Crom, and Stuart R. Levine, *The Leader in You: How
to Win Friends, Influence People and Succeed in a Changing World*
(New York: Pocket Books, 1993), 93.

p. 93   *Ninety-three percent of communication effectiveness:* Jacq Spence,
"Nonverbal Communication: How Body Language & Nonverbal
Cues Are Key," Lifesize (blog), February 18, 2020, lifesize.com/
blog/speaking-without-words/#:~:text=These%20studies%20
led%20Dr.,is%20"nonverbal"%20in%20nature.

Chapter 8: Demonstrating Your Solutions

p. 100   *Recent research from Bain & Company:* Eric Almquist, Jamie
Cleghorn, and Lori Sherer, "The B2B Elements of Value,"
Harvard Business Review, March–April 2018, hbr.org/2018/
03/the-b2b-elements-of-value.

p. 101   *Just having satisfied customers:* Ken Blanchard and Sheldon
Bowles, *Raving Fans! A Revolutionary Approach to Customer
Service* (London: HarperCollins, 1998), 12–13.

Chapter 9: Validating So People Believe Your Claims

p. 108   *Publicly traded companies that were designated:* "Ethisphere
Announces the 2021 World's Most Ethical Companies,"
Ethisphere, February 23, 2021, ethisphere.com/2021
-wme-announcement.

Chapter 11: Closing to Ask for the Appropriate Action

p. 128   *Often when you think you're at the end:* Fred Rogers, *The World
According to Mister Rogers: Important Things to Remember* (New
York: Hyperion, 2003), 40.

Chapter 12: Preparing for Sales Success

p. 129   *There's a famous scene: The Odd Couple,* directed by Gene Saks
(Hollywood, CA: Paramount Pictures, 1968).

p. 134   *our short-term memories can hold up to:* "The 5 Types of Memory
Everyone Has and Why They Matter," *The Healthy,* October 21,
2020, thehealthy.com/aging/mind-memory/memory-types/.

p. 134   *70,000 thoughts in a day:* "You Are Your Brain," *Healthy Brains*
(Cleveland Clinic), n.d., healthybrains.org/brain-facts/.

p. 134   *Fifty percent of the information:* Art Kohn, "Brain Science: The
Forgetting Curve—The Dirty Secret of Corporate Training,"
Learning Guild, March 13, 2014, learningguild.com/articles/
1379/brain-science-the-forgetting-curvethe-dirty-secret-of
-corporate-training.

p. 134   *But when people were taking notes:* Mark Murphy,
"Neuroscience Explains Why You Need to Write Down
Your Goals If You Actually Want to Achieve Them," *Forbes,*
April 15, 2018, forbes.com/sites/markmurphy/2018/04/15/
neuroscience-explains-why-you-need-to-write-down-your
-goals-if-you-actually-want-to-achieve-them.

p. 140   *I believe luck is preparation:* "Thought for Today: Luck," Oprah.com,
March 19, 2010, oprah.com/spirit/thought-for-today-luck.

Chapter 13: Ten Techniques for Outstanding Preparation

p. 145   *According to one survey:* "2018 B2B Buyers Survey Report: Sales Representatives Play Greater Role Within Critical 1–3 Month Active Buyer Timeframe," Demand Gen Report, 2018, demandgenreport.com/resources/reports/2018-b2b-buyers -survey-report.

p. 150   *Researchers agree that mental preparation:* James E. Driskell, Carolyn Copper, and Aidan Moran, "Does Mental Practice Enhance Performance?" *Journal of Applied Psychology* 79, no. 4 (1994): 481–92, dx.doi.org/10.1037//0021-9010.79.4.481.

p. 151   *What we think about "under the surface":* Brian Tracy, "Subconscious Mind Power Explained," Brian Tracy International, n.d., briantracy.com/blog/personal-success/ understanding-your-subconscious-mind/.

p. 154   *It doesn't matter what:* Barbara Reynolds, *And Still We Rise: Interviews with 50 Black Role Models* (Washington, DC: USA Today Books, 1988), 176.

Chapter 14: Sales Coaching

p. 172   *Coaching isn't therapy:* Claire Tristram, "Wanna Be a Player? Get a Coach!" *Fast Company*, October 31, 1996, fastcompany.com/ 27767/wanna-be-player-get-coach.

Chapter 15: The Emotionally Intelligent Salesperson

p. 175   *In any leadership or mentorship role:* Michael Bungay Stanier, *The Advice Trap: Be Humble, Stay Curious & Change the Way You Lead Forever* (Vancouver: Page Two, 2020).

p. 176   *Some researchers think this is because:* "Sensitivity to Criticism," GoodTherapy, August 14, 2019, goodtherapy.org/learn-about -therapy/issues/sensitivity.

p. 178   *However, research over the past few decades:* "New Study Shows Nice Guys Finish First," American Management Association, January 24, 2019, amanet.org/articles/new-study-shows-nice -guys-finish-first.

p. 182   *Emotionally intelligent people:* Travis Bradberry, *Emotional Intelligence Habits: A Powerful New Way to Increase Your Emotional Intelligence* (San Diego, CA: TalentSmart, 2023), 306.

Chapter 16: Self and Team Assessments

p. 196 *Consistently and overwhelmingly:* K. Anders Ericsson, Michael
        J. Prietula, and Edward T. Cokely, "The Making of an Expert,"
        Harvard Business Review, July–August 2007, hbr.org/2007/07/
        the-making-of-an-expert.

Conclusion

p. 205 *Living into our values:* "Dare to Lead List of Values," Brené
        Brown (website), n.d., brenebrown.com/resources/dare-to
        -lead-list-of-values.

Index

About Integrity Solutions

INTEGRITY SOLUTIONS has over five decades of experience providing excellent, award-winning sales training and coaching solutions in 130 countries and industries, including health care, financial services, manufacturing and industrial, energy and utilities, contact centers, agriculture, transportation, and more.

The sales performance experts at Integrity Solutions equip sales teams to rise and achieve their full potential by building trusted customer relationships grounded in integrity. The firm is the partner of choice for values-driven organizations and specializes in innovative sales, service, and coaching training solutions that fuel performance, grow talent, lift customers, and elevate leaders.

Integrity Solutions is consistently recognized annually as a Top Sales Training Company by both Selling Power and Training Industry, Inc., and the firm has received multiple Stevie Awards for Sales Training and Consulting excellence. ISA—the global Association of Learning Providers—recognized Integrity Solutions as their 2022 Business of the Year.

About the Authors

MIKE ESTERDAY first discovered his talent for sales when he ranked number one out of 6,000 sales professionals in his first sales role, and then recruited and managed hundreds of salespeople. Forty years later, Esterday is a sought-after coach, speaker, and leader in sales management and training. He has established multiple successful companies and is a founding partner and CEO of Integrity Solutions. A past board member of ISA, the global Association of Learning Providers, he is also a contributing member of the Forbes Business Council.

DEREK ROBERTS has built, trained, and coached sales teams and sales leaders for nearly thirty years. He is an executive coach, consultant, and professional speaker, but is quick to identify himself first and foremost as a sales professional. A partner with Integrity Solutions since 1999, Roberts also owns the consulting and training firm Roberts Business Group, which sells and distributes Integrity Solutions' products. He is coauthor of *Be a Mindsetter: The Essential Guide to Inspire, Influence and Impact Others*.

WE'RE
LISTENING

WE HOPE that *Listen to Sell* has ignited the inspiration, confidence, and motivation to achieve what you're truly capable of as a salesperson and sales leader. As with any professional development, it's a journey. We want to keep the conversation going and offer more opportunities to connect, learn, and grow.

Visit us online at listentosellbook.com and integritysolutions .com (or scan the QR code) for videos, articles, testimonials, podcasts, self-assessments, infographics, and upcoming events.

Consider group purchases of *Listen to Sell*. Whether for your team or for a conference or event, bulk discounts are available at listentosellbook.com.

Invite us to speak at an upcoming event. We offer conference keynotes, scheduled webinars, and podcasts on the strategies you discovered in this book and many more.

Bring us in with your team to uncover and sustain their true sales potential. If you have a large group eligible for our training, contact us at info@integritysolutions.com.

Share your thoughts about *Listen to Sell* and what you've learned from it on social media. Use the hashtags:

#ListenToSell
#IntegritySelling
#SalesMindset

Leave a review on your preferred book retailer's website. It will build our *Listen to Sell* community, and we greatly appreciate your feedback.

Connect with Mike and Derek:
linkedin.com/in/mikeesterday
linkedin.com/in/derekroberts1